SOFTBALL: SLOW AND FAST PITCH

About the Authors

Marian E. Kneer, Professor Emeritus of Physical Education, University of Illinois at Chicago, received her PhD from the University of Michigan. Dr. Kneer has had a long association with softball as a player in four ASA World Softball Championships, a member of the Joint International Rules Committee on Softball, a writer of numerous softball articles for the former Division of Girls and Women's Sports, and as a consultant for several softball filmstrips. She is a member of the Illinois ASA Softball Hall of Fame and the Illinois State University Athletic Hall of Fame. She has had extensive experiences as a high school physical education teacher and as a softball coach. Presently, Dr. Kneer is a physical education curriculum and instruction specialist and is coauthor of the book *Physical Education Instruction Techniques: An Individualized Humanistic Approach,* published by Prentice-Hall.

Charles McCord, having achieved success in teaching, coaching and competitive sports, again joins forces as coauthor with Dr. Kneer in this revision.

After earning his degree from Eastern Illinois University, he both taught and coached for two years at the high school level. For eighteen years he officiated competitive sports on both the high school and college level. During this time, he has conducted clinics overseas on softball for the men and women of the United States Armed Forces.

Besides his teaching and coaching accomplishments, he managed the nationally famous women's softball team, Lettes, of Caterpillar-Sunnyland and Pekin, Illinois, from 1947–72. During his tenure, the team qualified for the national tournament nineteen times.

Since 1952 he has held the position of State Softball Commissioner for the Illinois Amateur Softball Association and is also the chairperson of the National Hall of Fame Selection Committee. He has held this position since 1958.

Mr. McCord is a member of the Pan-American Committee for Softball and assisted in writing the procedure for selecting the players to represent the United States teams. He was elected president of the Amateur Softball Association in 1984, is a member of the Eastern Illinois University and Peoria Area Athletic Hall of Fame and Illinois ASA Hall of Fame.

SOFTBALL: SLOW AND FAST PITCH

Fifth Edition

Marian E. Kneer
Professor Emeritus, University of Illinois at Chicago

Charles L. McCord
Chairman, National Softball Hall of Fame Committee

 Wm. C. Brown Publishers

Book Team

Editor *Chris Rogers*
Developmental Editor *Cindy Kuhrasch*
Production Coordinator *Peggy Selle*

 Wm. C. Brown Publishers

President *G. Franklin Lewis*
Vice President, Publisher *George Wm. Bergquist*
Vice President, Publisher *Thomas E. Doran*
Vice President, Operations and Production *Beverly Kolz*
National Sales Manager *Virginia S. Moffat*
Advertising Manager *Ann M. Knepper*
Marketing Manager *Kathy Law Laube*
Production Editorial Manager *Colleen A. Yonda*
Production Editorial Manager *Julie A. Kennedy*
Publishing Services Manager *Karen J. Slaght*
Manager of Visuals and Design *Faye M. Schilling*

Consulting Editor
Physical Education
Aileene Lockhart
Texas Women's University

Sports and Fitness Series Evaluation Materials Editor
Jane A. Mott
Texas Women's University

Cover photo by Bob Coyle

Cover design by Jeanne Marie Regan

Copyright © 1966, 1976, 1980, 1987, 1991 by Wm. C. Brown Publishers. All rights reserved

Library of Congress Catalog Card Number: 89–81101

ISBN 0–697–10120–7

No part of this publication may be reproduced, stored in a retrieval system, or transmitted, in any form or by any means, electronic, mechanical, photocopying, recording, or otherwise, without the prior written permission of the publisher.

Printed in the United States of America by Wm. C. Brown Publishers, 2460 Kerper Boulevard, Dubuque, IA 52001

10 9 8 7 6 5 4 3 2

Contents

Preface   vii

What Softball Is Like   1

1

Facts for Enthusiasts   7

2

Language and Lore of the
Game   13

3

Offensive Skills   21

4

Defensive Skills   41

5

Defensive Position Play   63

6

Patterns of Play   89

7

Teaching, Coaching, and Managing   101

8

Rules and Unwritten Laws of the Game   107

9

Playing the Game   117

10

Umpiring and Scorekeeping 123

11

Questions and Answers   133
Index   141

Preface

Although softball is a well-established game, rules, equipment and strategies do slowly change over time. The fifth edition of *Softball Slow and Fast Pitch* reflects these changes. In addition the text has been refined and illustrations improved.

The purposes of this book are to assist all softball players of any age, beginners to advanced, to acquire knowledge and skills necessary for playing fast- or slow-pitch softball; to provide instructors, coaches and managers with substantive information about softball and suggestions for structuring meaningful and productive learning experiences; and to aid students of the game to learn how to umpire and keep score. Emphasis has been placed on skill analysis, error correction, values of softball and its place in our culture. Individual and group practice suggestions are included to foster improvement in performance.

Self-evaluation questions are distributed throughout the text. They afford the reader typical examples of the kinds of understanding and levels of skill that should be acquired as progress is made toward mastery of softball. The player should not only answer the printed questions but should pose additional ones as a self-check on learning. Since the order in which the content of the text is read and the teaching progression of the instructor are matters of individual choice, the evaluative materials are not positioned according to the presentation of given topics. In some instances the reader may find that he or she cannot respond fully and accurately to a question without more extensive reading or more playing experience. From time to time the reader should return to such troublesome questions until he or she is sure of the answers or has developed the skills called for, as the case may be.

Acknowledgments

I wish to thank the reviewers for this text: Robert Gwyn (North Carolina State University), Cheryl A. Kennedy (Slippery Rock University), M. Gene Lee (Metropolitan State College), Richard Raklovits (Western Michigan University), Beverly R. Sullivan (Pensacola Christian College), and Ron Peter (Windham, CT).

What Softball Is Like

1

You will be able to—

1. distinguish softball from baseball,
2. differentiate between fast-pitch and slow-pitch softball,
3. understand the general conduct of a softball game,
4. identify the playing areas of an official field,
5. identify equipment necessary for playing softball.

Softball is the largest participatory sport in the United States. Over thirty million Americans of all ages, size, ability and sex enjoy playing it informally at picnics, parks and recreation areas, and formally in a variety of leagues, conferences and tournaments at interscholastic, intercollegiate recreational, industrial and professional levels.

Softball is a variation of baseball that was originated by George Hancock of Chicago, Illinois, in 1887 to permit the popular game of baseball to be played indoors. He devised smaller playing dimensions to accommodate the larger and softer ball. The variation became so popular that the indoor game was brought outdoors and became known by a variety of names such as kittenball or mushball. Recreation agencies found the adaptation to be better suited and more appealing to all ages and both sexes than baseball, which required a heavier bat, smaller and harder ball, and a larger playing area. Softball, on the other hand, is played on a smaller diamond with a larger ball and a lighter bat. The pitcher pitches underhand instead of overhand. Base runners may not lead off base in some variations of the game, and a game consists of seven instead of nine innings. These changes provide a sport that is like baseball but can be played in a smaller area by men, women and children. It has become basically an amateur sport, whereas baseball includes professional as well as amateur play.[1]

Softball is a game for everyone. Power is required to hit the ball, yet accuracy in placing the ball so that a fielder cannot reach it can make up for lack of power. The varied playing situations require quick, intelligent decisions. The game calls for individual and team effort. Basic skills are throwing, catching, running and hitting. The game demands strenuous effort and yet provides sufficient rest periods. The equipment is relatively inexpensive, and the rules are easily adapted to various playing situations. Softball is one of the safest sports for participants of any age.

---

1. *Softball, A Game for Everyone* (Oklahoma City: Amateur Softball Association of America, 1977), p. 2.

Informal softball is played extensively with rules modified by the participants to suit the situation at picnics, in parks, in backyards or on the streets. The thrill of catching a ball or striking a ball with a bat is sought by many. The game is most often played officially by leagues comprised of several teams. These leagues may be sponsored by schools, playgrounds, recreation departments, churches or industrial organizations. The highly skilled players perform on teams that are usually sponsored by a business or industrial organization. The teams often travel considerable distances to seek comparable competition. The Amateur Softball Association (ASA) is the main governing body for softball in the United States. They have drawn up rules governing play for teams that wish to affiliate and to compete in metropolitan, state, regional, national and international competition. Many organizations sponsor softball leagues and adopt special rules for their play only.

Playing Field

The softball playing field is the space within which the ball may be legally played and fielded. This space must be clear and unobstructed within the prescribed fence distances and sidelines, which are called *foul lines*. This space is divided into two major areas, the *infield* and the *outfield*. The infield is the area containing the diamond formed by the placement of the bases. There are three bases and a home plate in the infield or diamond. The home plate is the starting point for play. The foul lines extend from home plate through first and third base to the fences. The outfield is the area between the infield and the fences. The distances between home plate and fences and from home plate to the bases vary between slow- and fast-pitch softball, between age levels of play and even between the gender of the participants. In general, there are four types of softball: 11- and 12-inch slow- and fast-pitch softball and 14- and 16-inch slow-pitch softball. The playing field, pitching distances and rules vary for each type of play and for youth, co-ed, collegiate and adult play.

Fast Pitch

The game of fast-pitch softball requires nine players on a team and ten if a designated hitter is to be used. Each team assigns players to certain defensive positions. These are pitcher, catcher, first baseman, second baseman, third baseman, shortstop, left fielder, center fielder and right fielder. The designated hitter does not play a defensive position but rather is assigned to bat for one of the defensive players who does not then bat. The players are stationed on a playing field that has a clear and unobstructed area within a radius of 225 feet for adult males, 200 feet for adult females, and a minimum of 175 feet from home plate between the foul lines for girls and boys under 15 years old. The batter stands at home plate and tries to hit a ball that is delivered by the pitcher. If the batter succeeds,

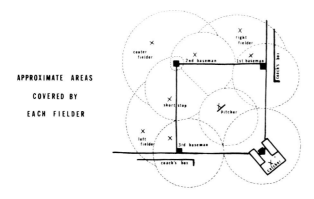

Figure 1.1
Diamond and defensive stations (fast pitch).

he or she tries to reach first base and eventually advance around the diamond until he or she returns to home plate. The players in the field try to prevent runners from scoring. Each time a runner crosses home plate, a run is scored. The team with the most runs after seven innings of play is the winner. Pitching dominates fast-pitch softball when it is played by highly skilled players.

The pitcher must deliver the ball underhand. The batter must decide whether or not to swing at the pitch. If the batter does not swing at it, the umpire judges whether the ball was delivered over the plate and between the batter's armpits and the top of his or her knees when the batter assumes a natural batting stance. This area is called the strike zone. If the pitch is in the strike zone, a strike is called. If it is not, a ball is called. If three strikes are called, the batter is declared out. If four balls are called, the batter is allowed to take first base. The batter attempts to hit the ball so that it will settle on fair ground in the infield or strike fair ground in the outfield. If the batted ball is hit outside of this area it is in foul territory and is called a foul ball. The first two are counted as strikes. When the ball is hit into fair territory, the batter and all other base runners try to reach as many bases as possible.

The defensive team members play positions within the boundary lines of the field and attempt to put batters and base runners out before they are able to complete the circuit of the bases.

Figure 1.1 illustrates the diamond and the defensive areas covered by each player. Outs occur when the batter strikes out, when a fly ball is caught, when the base is touched with the ball before the runner reaches it when forced to run because of a succeeding runner and when a runner is touched with the ball before reaching a base. Three outs retire the batting team. The fielding team is then given a chance to bat and to score runs. When each team has had a turn at bat, an inning has been completed.

Slow Pitch

Slow-pitch softball has in recent years shown tremendous growth. The major difference from fast-pitch softball is evident in the name itself. The pitcher is restricted to delivering the ball at a moderate speed with a perceptible arc from the time it leaves his or her hand until it reaches approximately 3 feet in front of home plate. Base runners may not steal bases, and a team consists of ten or eleven players. The extra players are called short fielder and extra hitter. The short fielder may play anywhere on the field. Extra hitters may not play on defense and may not be used in co-ed slow-pitch game. Bunting is illegal. Slow-pitch softball attracts more participants than fast-pitch softball because it is less physically demanding in terms of hitting, throwing and baserunning.

Slow-pitch was designed to permit more offensive action by making batting easier. However, the tenth player, the short fielder, is usually placed in the outfield to make place hitting more difficult. Although fast-pitch softball may make batting more difficult, a faster pitched ball goes farther when hit, and bunting a pitched ball and stealing bases are allowed, which increases offensive action. The two types of play result in differences in strategy, challenge and player interests. The major throwing, batting, catching and fielding techniques are used in both slow-pitch and fast-pitch softball.

Equipment

The minimum equipment necessary to play softball officially is a ball and a bat. However, players usually wear gloves or mitts depending upon their position. Fast-pitch adult catchers must wear a mask with a throat protector, and Junior Olympic catchers must wear a mask, throat protector, helmet, shinguards and body protector. However, in slow-pitch softball the only protection required of catchers is an approved batting helmet for players in Junior Olympic competition. Body protectors and shinguards are recommended for all catchers in fast-pitch play. All adult fast pitch and Junior Olympic fast- and slow-pitch offensive players must wear approved batting helmets.

What is the minimum equipment needed to play fast- or slow-pitch softball?

Shoes that provide traction with metal or rubber spikes attached to the sole and heel of the shoes are considered essential. However, no metal, hard plastic or polyurethane spikes are allowed in youth and co-ed play. Uniforms are optional but are often worn by teams in leagues and in highly skilled competition. More information about equipment is provided in Chapter Two.

The game of fast-pitch or slow-pitch softball provides enjoyment and challenge for persons of both sexes, all ages and varied skill levels. A great deal of force and control is necessary to hit or throw the ball within the limits of the playing space. Players must learn to absorb that force in order to catch or stop the ball. Timing and flow are integral aspects of the game. Timing is needed for executing plays or swinging at the pitched ball. Flow of movement is essential for combining a series of skills for a single execution, such as pitching or executing a double play.

How do slow- and fast-pitch softball compare in the following: number of players; amount of action in the game; delivery of pitches; baserunning; and bunting regulations?

References

Houseworth, Steven D. and Rivkin, Francine. *Coaching Softball Effectively.* Champaign, Illinois: Human Kinetic Press, 1985.

Meyer, Robert G. *The Complete Book of Softball.* New York, New York: Leisure Press, 1984, Chapter 1.

National Association for Girls' and Women's Sports. *Softball Guide.* Reston, Virginia.: American Alliance for Health, Physical Education, Recreation and Dance (published biannually).

Official Guide and Rule Book. Oklahoma City, Oklahoma: Amateur Softball Association (published yearly).

Official's Manual: Softball. Rittler, Kathy. West Point, New York: Leisure Press, 1982, Chapter 3.

Softball, A Game for Everyone. Oklahoma City, Oklahoma: Amateur Softball Association, 1977.

Facts for Enthusiasts

2

Enthusiasts need to know the kind of equipment to purchase and how to care for it. In addition, information about the possibilities of participation in tournaments will enhance a player's appreciation of the game. You will be able to—

1. select and care for equipment, and
2. appreciate the wide acceptance of softball.

Selection and Care of Equipment

The minimum equipment necessary to play softball officially is a ball and a bat. Bases may be makeshift, and official dimensions modified.

Bats

The rules permit a variety of materials to be used in manufacturing official bats: wood, laminated wood, plastic, bamboo and metal. In addition, there are several unofficial plastic bats that are hollow, lightweight and do not present a hazard to students or to gym floors. A wide selection of bats with differing size grips and barrels should be available. The bat is made of one piece of hardwood or formed from woods bonded together with plastic, bamboo or metal. The surface must be smooth and free of burrs, rivets or other hazards. It is not more than 34 inches long or more than $2\frac{1}{8}$ inches in diameter at its largest part and has a safety grip of cork, tape or composition material. A safety knob of a minimum of $\frac{1}{4}$ inch protruding at a 90-degree angle from the handle must be included on all bats.

Choose a bat that feels balanced and seems to be the proper weight for you to swing with power and whip. A heavy, tapered bat is often used by power hitters. The "bottleneck" bat is used for sharp hits out of the infield or for bunting. Bats made from ash woods tend to be lighter than hickory bats. The aluminum bat is now the most preferred bat because of its durability and low cost. It is often used by players because off-center contacts seem to maintain more power. On the other hand, many players still prefer the wooden bat because they believe they can "whip" it better and it sounds more solid upon contact with the ball.

Balls

Softballs vary in size according to type of play. The 12-inch ball is used in fast- and slow-pitch softball and must be a minimum of 11⅞ inches and a maximum of 12⅛ inches in circumference and be a minimum of 6¼ ounces and a maximum of 7 ounces in weight. Fast-pitch play uses a ball with white stitches and slow-pitch, red stitches. Sixteen-inch slow-pitch play uses a 16-inch ball circumference, which may range from 15¾ to 16¼ inches and be 9 to 10 ounces in weight. An 11-inch ball is used in women's slow-pitch, co-ed slow-pitch (for women batters only), and all girls' Junior Olympic slow-pitch play. The core of the ball is made of long fiber kapok, a mixture of cork and rubber, a polyurethane mixture, or other materials approved by the ASA. It may be hand- or machine-wound, with fine quality twisted yards, and covered with latex or rubber cement. The cover is made from either horsehide, cowhide, synthetic material or other material approved by the ASA.

Softballs are closely controlled by the rules as to weight, diameter, contents, cover and stitching. Be certain when buying softballs that they are marked "Official Softball." The brand name of the balls you purchase depends upon personal choice. Most players like to play with a ball that "feels" light; however, these balls often are not durable.

Fleece balls and plastic balls are recommended for primary-age children, but in junior high school, regular fast-pitch softballs should be used. If the ball seems too hard, a rubber-covered, soft softball may be more desirable. Teams should use regulation softballs. Tests are made each year by the Amateur Softball Association Equipment Standards Committee to determine conformity to the rules.

Batting Helmets

All adult fast-pitch and Junior Olympic fast- and slow-pitch offensive players must properly wear approved batting helmets. Helmets on a team are to be of similar color with double earflaps. The helmets must have safety features equal to or greater than those provided by the full plastic cap with padding on the inside.

Gloves and Mitts

There are many styles of gloves and mitts. Mitts do not have fingers. Individual differences in hand size and comfort of the glove will determine the style you purchase. Only the catcher and the first baseman may wear mitts, and the rules spell out the specific regulations concerning their pattern. The webbing of the glove may not be more than 5 inches. The pitcher's glove must be of one color and not white or gray. Multicolor gloves are unacceptable.

Most players prefer a baseball glove with a large pocket to gloves specially constructed for softball use. Baseball catchers' mitts do not work well for catchers' mitts. Usually, first basemen's mitts are used by catchers. Padding is not too

Figure 2.1
Softball equipment.

important in softball gloves or mitts, but the softness of the leather is important. Horse-, cow-, or elkhide are excellent leather coverings. The palms should be oiled or greased. At the end of the season, mitts and gloves should be oiled and stored with a ball or a wad of paper wrapped in the pocket.

Why is the aluminum bat often preferred over the wood bat?

Masks and Protectors

The rules for fast and slow pitch vary concerning the use of masks and protectors. In fast-ball play masks with a throat protector must be worn by all catchers, and youth catchers must also wear a protective helmet, body protector and shinguards. These protective devices are recommended for slow pitch but not required. Softball masks are made much lighter than baseball masks. They can be purchased with sponge rubber padding or with hair padding covered with leather. Both are excellent, and the selection is a matter of individual preference. Body protectors should be made especially for softball and be only waist long. Light-colored duck filled with kapok is the material commonly used for protectors.

Shoes

Shoes must be worn by all players. A shoe shall be considered official if it is made with either canvas, leather or other similar material. The soles may be smooth or have soft or hard rubber cleats. Adult players in non-co-ed play prefer to wear spiked shoes for better traction on the playing ground. Metal sole and heel cleats must be less than ¾ inches. Rounded metal spikes are illegal. No metal, hard plastic or polyurethane spikes are permitted for youth or co-ed play.

Bases, Home Plate, Pitcher's Plate

The regulation home plate is five-sided and made of rubber. The pitcher's plate is constructed of wood or rubber; it is 24 inches long and 6 inches wide. The distance of the pitching plate varies from 46 feet to 35 feet from home plate. Consult the rule book for your type of play. Bases covered with canvas or other suitable material are 15 inches square. They are placed 60 feet apart and are fastened in place.

In official games, home and pitcher's plates are rubber, and the bases are made with a canvas cover. Official play requires that all bases and plates be secured to the ground.

Specific regulations determine whether or not a softball is "official." When is a red-stitched ball used? a ball with a 12-inch circumference? a ball with an 11-inch circumference?

The Game Today

For almost one hundred years softball has been a prime recreational and competitive sport in the United States. Today, it has a home in over fifty countries in the world. Over thirty million adults and youngsters in the United States and over twelve million in other parts of the world play softball. Each summer thousands of tournaments are held sponsored by schools, churches, armed forces, fraternal clubs, recreation agencies, industries, the Amateur Softball Association (ASA), the United States Slow-Pitch Softball Association (USSPSA) and interscholastic and intercollegiate associations. Competition on the international level is growing. Women led the way with the first tournament in Australia in 1965, and men soon followed in 1967 in Mexico. These games are played every four years. It is expected that softball will soon be included as an Olympic sport. Softball is an official sport of the Pan-American Games. Don Porter, executive director of the Amateur Softball Association, states: "There is hardly a man or woman in the United States who didn't at one time play softball."[1] Playing field facilities are insufficient to fill the demand for playing softball, especially slow-pitch softball. Rules are printed in fifteen different languages.

---

1. Don E. Porter, "Softball—Past, Present and Future," *Journal of Health, Physical Education Recreation* 42 (May 1971):36–37.

Figure 2.2
Softball Hall of Fame.

The Amateur Softball Association (ASA) is organized to promote softball and to provide clinics and information designed to improve play as well as to organize tournaments on a local, district, state, regional, national and world basis. More than 220,000 teams are involved in ASA adult programs for both fast-pitch and slow-pitch softball. Each year more than a thousand invitational and championship tournaments are conducted at all levels of skill and for both sexes. The ASA Youth Program involves over seven hundred thousand children.

In 1957 the Amateur Softball Association developed a Softball Hall of Fame. Selections are made on the basis of documented evidence of outstanding performance and contributions to the game on a national level. The headquarters for the Amateur Softball Association and the Softball Hall of Fame are located in Oklahoma City, Oklahoma. In addition to the above services the ASA provides the following:

Aids and clinics for umpires, coaches and players
Assistance in local league organization and play
Publications (rules, guides, monthly newspaper and national magazine)
Free literature and instructional films

The International Softball Congress (ISC) is another fast-pitch-only organization. It sponsors tournaments with winners advancing to a world playoff and publishes an annual yearbook. The International Softball Federation (ISF) is composed of a group of national softball organizations that coordinate softball development and international competition. ISF encourages growth of softball on a worldwide basis.

The National Association for Girls and Women's Sports (NAGWS) and the National Association for Sport and Physical Education of the American Alliance for Health, Physical Education, Recreation and Dance promote softball in educational institutions. The NAGWS sponsors a Softball Committee that biannually publishes a Softball Guide with instructional articles, officiating information, rules and media resources. Softball is usually included in the physical education curriculum from elementary school through college.

The National Federation of State High School Sport organizes high school tournaments.

What opportunities are provided in your community for tournament play and for softball clinics?

Several attempts have been made to professionalize the game. An attempt was made for women in the late forties and fifties and again for both men and women in the late seventies. None of these attempts have been successful over an extended period of time.

References

ASA Softball. Oklahoma City, Oklahoma: Amateur Softball Association (nationally circulated magazine).

Balls and Strikes. Oklahoma City, Oklahoma: Amateur Softball Association (monthly newspaper).

Jones, Billie J. and Murray, Mary Jo. *Softball Concepts for Coaches and Teachers.* Dubuque, Iowa: Wm. C. Brown Company Publishers, 1978, Chapters 1 and 2.

Meyer, Robert G. *The Complete Book of Softball.* New York, New York: Leisure Press, 1984, Chapter 1.

Language and Lore of the Game

3

Softball is a "peoples" game that has endured for almost a hundred years. As such it has developed a history, a lore and a language. You will be able to—

1. appreciate and understand the history of softball, and
2. understand and apply common softball terms.

The concept of striking an object and reaching a destination before being "put out" can be traced to England. Early games based on this concept were called "Rounders" or "Town Ball." The early colonists adapted "Rounders" into a game called "One Old Cat." Folklore credits Abner Doubleday in 1839 as having scratched the first baseball diamond in the dust at Cooperstown, New York, and outlined general playing rules. It was then, according to legend, that baseball and its many variations started to grow.

Softball is the most famous offspring of baseball, our national pastime. On a Thanksgiving afternoon in 1887 the Chicago Farragut Boat Club devised and played an indoor game similar to baseball. A boxing glove and broom were used as a ball and bat. The afternoon's fun offered promise, a promise fulfilled by George W. Hancock, a member of the club, who developed rules and equipment. He produced a larger, softer ball and a bat with a smaller batting surface.

Early organization of game play began in Minneapolis, Minnesota. Lewis Rober, a member of the municipal fire department, made the first "kittenball," or softball, by hand. The firemen amused themselves by playing with it in their free time. The first softball league was organized in Minneapolis in 1900, and the first published rules covering the sport appeared in Minneapolis in 1906. During the next twenty years the game was played both indoors and outdoors. It was called mushball, kittenball and pumpkinball. Because the game was less dangerous than baseball, women readily took to it. The game was called "softball" by Walter A. Hakanson, a YMCA Director from Denver, Colorado, in 1926. That name was officially adopted in 1933.

Since indoor space was not always available, the game began to be played outdoors more and more. Around 1930 Leo H. Fischer and M. J. Pauley of Chicago adapted the game so that it could be played outdoors. They conducted tournaments that were so successful they were able to convince the 1933 Chicago World's Fair to sponsor a national tournament for men and for women.

Thousands of unemployed adults of the 1932–33 depression years found the game a satisfying way to use excess leisure time. When they finally found employment, they took the game with them and encouraged their employers to sponsor industrial leagues and teams of highly skilled players. The first national

13

tournament pointed up a need for greater organization. In 1934 all organizations sponsoring tournaments met and formed the Amateur Softball Association. At the same time a Joint Rules Committee was formed to standardize rules. Previous to the formation of this committee, the National Recreation Association and the American Physical Education Association published their own set of rules.

The Amateur Softball Association organized softball into city, state and regional associations as well as industrial, city, co-ed and church leagues. Regional champions competed in a national tournament. Early championship teams came from the Midwest. Since that time champions have come from all different parts of the United States. The national fast-pitch men's and women's championship teams compete in a World Championship tournament. Many teams were and still are sponsored by business and industrial concerns. In recent years these teams have been considered national powers:

1. Steele's Silver Bullets. A 12-inch slow-pitch team from Crofton, Ohio.
2. Starpath-Kink's Glass. A 12-inch super slow-pitch team from Monticello, Kentucky.
3. Sioux City Penn Corporation. A 12-inch fast-pitch team from Iowa. They were the 1988 ISC champions.
4. Pete's Hideaway Whips. Chicago, Illinois. The 1988 16-inch ASA Slow-Pitch Major National Champions.
5. Trans-Aire. Men's Major Fast-Pitch 1988 National Champions from Elkhart, Indiana.
6. Hi Ho Brakettes. The women's Major Fast-Pitch 1988 Champions from Stratford, Connecticut.
7. Spooks. Women's Major Slow-Pitch 1988 Champions from Anoka, Minnesota.
8. South Florida Club. The co-ed Slow-Pitch Champions from Harbor Island, Florida.

During World War II, softball experienced a brief departure from amateur to professional play for some girls and women. It was born out of concern for the restricted baseball activity because of the war. In Chicago a Women's Professional League was formed, and shortly afterward, P. K. Wrigley gave support to a Midwest version of women's professional play in a game that was essentially a blend of softball and baseball. Both of these attempts died shortly after the end of the war.

Fast-pitch softball dominated the game from 1940 to 1960. The tendency for excellent pitching to result in low-scoring games gave rise to increasing interest in two variations of the game: slow-pitch softball with a regular-size ball and slow-pitch softball with a larger-size ball. These variations prohibited base stealing, required the ball to be pitched slowly and permitted two extra players. Slow-pitch softball attracts about 70 percent of softball participants because it lessens the impact of the pitcher on the game outcome and lessens the need for speed on the bases. Consequently the games become more offensive and provide more opportunity for player involvement.

Figure 3.1
Hall of Fame Stadium.

Softball provides physical activity that permits maximum social interaction. It is fun, relaxing, challenging, active and rarely dangerous. It is no wonder that softball has such wide appeal.

As both baseball and softball were played experts developed the game by devising certain playing techniques, and some of their inventions resulted in the formation of new rules. Bill Cummings of Massachusetts developed spins on pitches by the skips and turns he observed when flinging clamshells into the ocean. Paul "Windmill" Watson of Arizona developed the circular windup and the fast pitch. John "Cannonball" Baker of Wisconsin invented the figure-eight windup. These developments resulted in increasing the pitching distances and prohibiting some of the windups.

The National Softball Hall of Fame was established by the ASA in 1957 and is located in Oklahoma City, Oklahoma. Both men and women players are eligible to be selected. Over sixty members have been inducted, which also includes founders, executives and umpires. Visitors may view the historical development of the game, see the pictures of great players and obtain information about their achievements. Some of the famous men in the Softball Hall of Fame are Harold Gears, Sam Elliott, Al Linde, Bernie Kampschmidt, Dizzy Kirkendall, Jim Ramage, Clarence Miller, John Baker, Warren Gerber, Hugh Johnson, Bill West, John Hunter, Tom Castle, Ben Crane, Ray Stephenson, Don Ropp, Jim Chambers, John Spring, Jerry Curtis, Charles Justice, Harvey Sterkel, Robert Kuykendal and John Anquillare. Women members of the Hall of Fame include Amy Peralta, Marie Wadlow, Betty Grayson, Ruth Sears, Nina Korgan, Marjorie Law, Kay Rich, Margaret Dobson, Bertha Tickey, Gloria May, Donna Lopiano, Joan Joyce and Lorene Ramsey. Slow-pitch "greats" are Myron Reinhardt, Frank DeLuca, Don Rardin, Alberta Sims, Ida Hopkins and Eddie Zolna.

As a tribute to these stars, the ASA has built the Hall of Fame Stadium located on the grounds of their headquarters site in Oklahoma City, Oklahoma. It is considered one of the finest softball stadiums in the world.

In addition, the ASA sponsors state Hall of Fames, and the ISC maintains a Hall of Fame in Kimberly, Wisconsin. Many local areas have developed their own softball Hall of Fame for any and all types of play.

Common Softball Terms

Most of the terms used in softball are taken from baseball. In most cases these terms simply explain the situation or name the person or item. Some of the terms seem to have little relationship to the situation defined, but there is usually some interesting lore about them.

Altered bat   A bat that has been physically changed so that it no longer meets legal standards.

Appeal play   A violation of the rules that must be called to the umpire's attention for a ruling. Appeal situations result from leaving a base before a fly ball is caught, not touching a base or batting out of order.

Assist   A fielding credit to a player who helps a teammate make a putout.

Away   The number of outs. "Two away" means the same as "two outs."

Backstop   Another name for the catcher and also the term given to a fence behind home plate.

Back-up   A position taken by a fielder behind the player attempting to field the ball to possibly play the ball if it gets past the first fielder.

Bag   The base.

Balk   A term applied to making a motion to pitch without immediately delivering the ball to the batter. If a balk is committed, a ball is called on the batter, and the base runners are given one additional base.

Base on balls   When four balls are called on the batter.

Base path   An imaginary path 3 feet wide on each side of a direct line between the bases.

Bases loaded, or Bases full   Base runners on every base.

Batter's box   An area on each side of home plate that is 7 feet long and 3 feet wide. The batter must stand within that area when batting.

Battery   The pitcher and the catcher. They are given that name because they really are the "power source" for action.

Batting order   Official sequence in which the batters will appear at the plate to bat.

Bean ball   A ball pitched too close to the batter's head.

Beat out   To reach a base on a slowly hit ball or a bunt.

Blocked ball   A batted or thrown ball that is interfered with by someone not officially in the game.

Blooper   A batted ball that arches over the heads of the infielders and drops just in front of the outfielders.

Bobble   Juggling the ball while attempting to catch it.

Box   The batter's area, the catcher's area and the coaches' area. All are officially measured and described in the rules.

16   *Chapter 3*

Box score   The description of the game that is condensed by the use of symbols. This name was given because the scorekeepers are assigned to an area referred to as a box.

Bunt   A weakly tapped ball that is directed toward the foul lines between home plate and first base and home plate and third base.

Catch   A ball that is batted or thrown and which goes directly to the fielder's glove or hand and is controlled.

Catcher's box   The area legally designated behind the batter in which the catcher is confined until the pitcher releases the ball.

Change of pace   The varying of the speed of a pitched ball.

Chopper   A batted ball that bounces high.

Chucker   The pitcher.

Circuit clout   A home run. The batter "clouts" the ball so far that he/she can circle all the bases.

Clean the bases   To hit a home run with base runners on.

Cleanup   The fourth hitter in the batting order. This name is given because he/she is the best hitter and most able to bring runners home.

Count   The number of called balls and strikes.

Crowd the plate   Standing close to the plate.

Cut   To swing at the ball.

Cutoff   Interception of a thrown ball made to put out an advancing runner to allow for changing the purpose of the throw if it appears to be unsuccessful.

Cycle   Hitting a single, double, triple and a home run in one game by one batter.

Dead ball   A ball no longer in play.

Designated hitter   A player who can only bat for a designated defensive player. (A fast-pitch-only option.)

Diamond   The area formed by the four bases.

Double play   Two outs usually resulting from one batted ball.

Down   Denotes the number of outs—similar to "away."

Earned run   A run that was scored through offensive play rather than an error.

Error   A defensive misplay.

Extra-base hit   A batted ball on which the batter reaches more than one base other than on an error.

Extra hitter   A player who can only bat. This player does not play or replace a defensive position. (A slow-pitch non-co-ed game option.)

Fair ball   Any legally batted ball that is touched or that stops in fair territory between home and first and home and third base, or which lands in fair territory and does not cross the foul line until after it passes first or third base.

Fan   To strike out.

Fielder's choice   A play in which the fielder elects to put out a base runner rather than the batter.

Fly ball   A batted ball hit into the air.

Language and Lore of the Game   17

Foot in bucket The batter steps away from the plate with his/her forward foot.

Force-out An out occurring when the defensive player in possession of the ball merely touches the base before the runner, who must move to that base because of the batter's becoming a base runner, reaches it.

Foul ball A ball hit outside of fair territory.

Foul tip A batted ball that goes directly to the catcher and is caught. A strike is called.

Four bagger A home run.

Free trip A base on balls.

Full count Three balls and two strikes.

Fungo A ball hit by tossing the ball from the hand and then hitting it. Fungo hitting is used to provide fielding practice.

Grand slam Home run with the bases loaded. Taken from the bridge term meaning the best you can get.

Groove The middle of the strike zone.

Grounder A batted ball that hits the ground as soon as it leaves the bat.

Hit To take a turn batting or to hit the ball so as to enable the batter to reach first base safely other than on an error or a base on balls.

Hit away Batter swinging for a hit rather than a bunt.

Hit batsman A batter hit by a pitched ball.

Hit the dirt To slide or to pull away from a bean ball.

Hole Area not covered by a defensive player. Holes result from shifts in positions.

Hot corner Third base.

Illegally batted ball A ball that is struck by an illegal bat or by the batter while outside the batter's box. Batter is called out.

Illegally caught ball A ball that is caught by the fielder's clothing, cap or mask. Base runners are allowed two bases on a thrown ball and three on a batted ball.

Infield Fair territory bounded by and including the base paths.

Infield fly rule Applies to a situation when a batter hits a fly ball that can be caught in the infield or shallow outfield and runners are on first and second or on all the bases and there are less than two outs. The batter is called out whether the ball is caught or not. Runners may advance at their own risk of being put out if the ball is dropped.

Innings A division of the game whereby each team has a turn at batting.

Interference An act of an offensive play that hinders a defensive player's attempt to execute a play.

Keystone sack Second base.

Lay one down To bunt.

Lead off The first batter up at the beginning of the game and/or inning.

Line drive A batted ball that travels in a straight line.

Mask Device worn by the catcher and umpires to protect their faces against foul balls or the bat.

Obstruction An act by a defensive player that hinders the movement of an offensive player around the bases.

Out The retirement of a batter or base runner during play.

Outfield The fair territory beyond the infield.

Outside pitch Pitched ball that misses the strike zone on the side away from the batter. It is an inside pitch if it misses on the side near the batter.

Overrun To run beyond the base.

Overthrow To throw above the baseman or fielder's head.

Pass A walk.

Passed ball A legally delivered ball that should have been controlled by the catcher with ordinary effort.

Pick-off To trap a runner off base.

Pinch hitter A substitute hitter. So named because often the hitter is put in when a team is losing or in a "pinch."

Pinch runner A substitute who is put in a game to replace a slow or injured runner on base. The replaced runner is then out of the game.

Pitchout A pitch purposely thrown wide of the plate so that the batter cannot hit it.

Pivot foot A foot that the pitcher keeps in constant touch with the pitching rubber until the ball is released. Failure to do so results in a ball being called.

Pop up A short, high fly in or near the infield.

Protest A complaint by a team that a playing rule has not been correctly applied. If upheld, the game may be replayed from the point of the error.

Pull hitter A hitter who tends to hit the ball too soon and then sharply follows through.

Putout When a batter or base runner flies or is thrown out.

RBI Runs batted in.

Relay man A player who catches a ball from another fielder for possible additional play or redirection.

Sacrifice bunt Advancing a base runner by forcing out the batter.

Sacrifice fly A fly ball that is caught, with less than two outs, and which allows a base runner to score.

Scratch hit A weak hit.

Shoestring catch A low diving catch by an outfielder. This term is used because the fielder literally catches the ball off his or her shoestrings.

Southpaw Left-handed pitcher or batter. Most ball fields are laid out with pitcher facing west; thus his/her left hand would face south.

Squeeze Advancing a runner from third by bunting.

Steal To advance to another base after the ball leaves the pitcher's hand and before he/she is in position to pitch again.

Straight away Normal defensive and hitting pattern.

Stuff Quality and quantity of the types of pitches used by the pitcher.

Tag To touch a base with the ball in hand before a runner arrives or to touch the runner with ball in hand.

Texas leaguer Weak fly that lands safely.

Three bagger   A three-base hit.

Trap   A ball that is caught immediately after it hits the ground.

Triple play   Three outs resulting from one batted ball.

Two bagger   A two-base hit.

Wait out   Strategy by the batter employed to insure hitting only good pitches but especially contrived to obtain a base on balls.

Walk   Occurs when four balls are called on the batter. The batter is then entitled to go to first base.

Wild pitch   An inaccurately delivered pitch that the catcher has little or no chance of stopping.

Can you define the following terms: bobble, fan, fielder's choice, hot corner?

References

Amateur Softball Association. *Softball Rules Guide*. Oklahoma City, Oklahoma.

Meyer, Robert G. *The Complete Book of Softball*. New York, New York: Leisure Press, 1984, Chapter 4.

Official Guide and Rule Book. Oklahoma City, Oklahoma: Amateur Softball Association, 1984.

Porter, Don E. "Softball—The Game Everyone Plays." *Holiday Inn International Magazine* (July–August 1974):45–46.

Offensive Skills

4

Softball is a fast-moving game that requires speed in running, agility in fielding, accuracy in hitting and throwing. The degree of mastery in applying these essential fundamentals to specific techniques of batting, fielding, throwing and baserunning will determine the ultimate enjoyment to be derived from playing the game. Since it takes the ball about one-third to one-half second to reach the batter from the pitcher's hand and about three seconds for a runner to run from one base to another in fast-pitch play, it is apparent that the offensive team must develop sufficient skill to bat and run bases with skill, power and speed. Although slow-pitch play gives the batter a bit more time, offensive skills are still important to develop.

Batting

Instructional Objectives

You will be able to—

1. hit pitched balls into fair territory,
2. bunt pitched balls that will roll slowly in fair territory near the foul line,
3. hit pitched balls into the desired areas,
4. analyze batting errors and apply corrective procedures.

No matter how well you can field, run, or throw, your value to a team will be considerably reduced if you do not have ability in batting. If you can't hit, you can't score, and if you can't score, you can't win. There are many different styles of batting. If one style seems to bring more success than another, adopt that style. The first step is to select a bat that is the proper length, weight and style for your body-build, strength and type of swing. Generally, short, small players select lighter and shorter bats, and taller and heavier players choose longer and heavier ones. The bat should feel balanced in your hands. It should be heavy enough to add force to the swing but light enough to permit wrist whip action.

Grip

There are three types of grips—long, medium and short or "choke." Regardless of the length of the grip, the bat is held with the hands together and with the fingers and thumbs wrapped around the handle. Your dominant hand is placed above the non-dominant hand. The second joints of the fingers of your top hand

LONG GRIP

Long or *power grip.* Hands near knob to increase leverage and to add force or when the pitch is slow.

MEDIUM GRIP

Medium or *average grip.* Lower hand is an inch or two up from the knob to obtain both power and accuracy.

CHOKE GRIP

Choke grip. Lower hand is placed three to four inches from knob to shorten leverage and gain control. Use when place hitting, or the pitcher has a fast, fast ball.

Figure 4.1
Batting grips.

should line up somewhere between the second and base joints of the fingers of your lower hand. Grasp the bat firmly but relaxed until you begin to swing. The distance between the knob of the bat and your lower hand on the handle influences the amount of power and control. There are three positions or grips: long or power, medium and choke or short. Which is used is a matter of personal preference, skill and game situation.

What is this grip called? When and why would you use it? (Show illustration of long grip.)

Stance

Batters use a variety of stances: close or away, short or deep, open or closed. Close or away refers to the distance the feet are from home plate. Short or deep refers to the distance the feet are in the batter's box. Open and closed refers to the position of the front foot in relation to home plate. The stance is open if the foot is further away from the plate than the rear foot and closed, if it is closer. The stance you use should make you feel comfortable and allow you to hit the balls thrown in the strike zone with accuracy and power.

Figure 4.2
Batting stance.

Figure 4.3
Side view of stance.

Figure 4.4
Rear view of stance.

In slow pitch, if the arc of the ball is less than 7 or 8 feet, it is better to move up and away to avoid "golfing" or "chopping" at the ball.

The distance you should stand from the plate can be measured and adjusted by bending slightly from the waist and placing the top of the bat on the outside corner of the plate while holding the bat with your regular grip. You should feel comfortable and balanced.

1. Stand facing the plate, feet parallel with the ground and shoulder-distance apart.
2. Non-dominant shoulder and head face the pitcher.
3. Knees should be relaxed and slightly bent.
4. Bat is held off the shoulder.
5. Arms are held away from the body so they are free to move.
6. Forward arm is held fairly level with the ground.
7. Raise back arm a bit to permit better leverage.
8. Eyes on the ball.

The Swing

The key to successful hitting is a well-timed and smooth swing that is consistently executed and accurately centered on the ball. Practice and concentration are needed to always "hit downward and through the ball."

There are many different styles of batting. However, the stride, pivot and arm action are crucial to successful hitting.

Figure 4.5
The swing.

1. Shift weight back as the pitch is released and take a low stride forward about 8 to 12 inches with lead foot. The timing of this action depends upon the expected speed of the ball. Keep the rear foot firm. Do not transfer weight forward until the bat begins to move forward.
2. Pivot on the ball of the rear foot.
3. Rotate the hips upon completion of the stride and keep eyes on the ball.
4. Bring hands and bat forward and extend the forward arm as you snap the wrists just before contact with the ball, then roll hands over.
5. Hit through the center of the ball as you bring the bat around in a full follow-through.
6. Keep the hips, shoulders and bat as level as possible.

The swinging action is like a coiling and uncoiling around a central axis, the spine. The swing is a rhythmical progressive movement starting with the pivot of the hips and shoulders, continuing with the arms and wrists. This coiling and uncoiling along with the back arm provides the power while the forward arm gives guidance to the swing. The rear leg supports the initial unleashing of the power and the front leg becomes the support for the transfer of power behind the ball.

Place-Hitting

The number or position of base runners as well as the position of the infield often leaves "holes" or openings between the fielders. A clever hitter knows how to bat into that area. Effective placements of the batted ball can be achieved by adjusting the time that the ball is hit, the position of the feet and the follow-through of the bat.

If you wish to bat the ball to the left side of the field, try to contact the ball in front of the body in order to shorten the arc of the swing. Your wrists should break sharply, causing a forceful follow-through to "pull" the ball to the side on

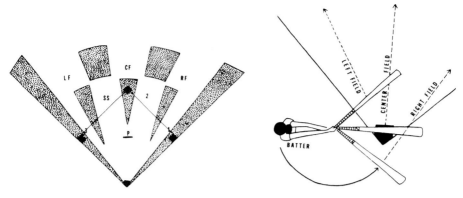

Figure 4.6
Place-hitting areas.

Figure 4.7
Place-hitting techniques.

which you are hitting. To hit the ball to center field, try to contact the ball directly opposite your body and follow-through naturally. To hit the ball to right field, try to contact the ball a little past the center of the body; let your follow-through angle the bat to right field. It is also possible to achieve placement of the ball by adjusting your stance, but this method permits the defense to become aware of your intentions and thus take preventive measures. If the pitcher is extremely fast or deceptive, it may not be possible to control the placement of the ball by these measures. In such situations the batter should "go with the pitch." Going with the pitch means that if the ball is outside, it is hit to that side of the field. To hit a long fly ball, grip the bat with a long grip, swing with full force, and try to follow-through slightly upward. To avoid hitting a ground ball, strike only at pitches above the waist.

When the pitcher has a great deal of speed, "choke" your grip on the bat in order to shorten the arc and permit a faster swing. Since this action results in decreased leverage, the power behind the ball will be lessened, but the accuracy of the hit will be increased.

Place-hitting ability is a definite asset to a team. Every good player should develop skill in this advanced technique.

Hit-and-Run

This technique is used to advance a base runner two or more bases, and at the same time it permits a ground ball, which normally would be fielded, to become a base hit. The hit-and-run play is most often used when there is a runner on first base. As soon as the ball leaves the pitcher's hand the runner on first base runs full speed to the next base. This action forces the second baseman to move to cover second base, thereby opening up a defensive "hole." The batter tries to place the ball into that "hole." Whenever this play is attempted by the offensive team, a gamble is taken that a sharp line drive will not be hit directly to a fielder, which would result in a double or triple play. Hit-and-run skill is difficult to master.

Offensive Skills

Figure 4.8
Hit-and-run play.

Bunting

Bunting is an essential skill for any fast-pitch softball player. A bunt is a batted ball that is not hit with a full swing. The bat is not swung at the ball but is placed in the way of the ball and allowed to "give" slightly in the hands, thus causing the ball to lose force. This action allows the ball to be placed approximately 10 to 20 feet from the plate and as near the base line as possible.

The ball is bunted to advance a base runner or as an attempt to get a base hit. Bunting to advance a base runner is called *sacrificing*. The sacrifice bunt draws the first baseman, pitcher and third baseman in toward the plate to field the ball, which forces the ball to be thrown to first base thus permitting the base runner to advance. A variation of the sacrifice bunt is the *squeeze bunt,* which is designed to score a base runner from third base. There are two techniques for bunting for a base hit: *drag bunting* and *push bunting.* Each of these requires surprise, proper placement and a fast sprint to first base to be successful. The drag bunt is placed along the first base line as the batter begins to run to first base. Because of this placement, drag bunting is best executed by left-handed batters. The push bunt is placed between the incoming fielders with enough speed to force the ball by them.

A great deal of the success of the bunt depends on the surprise element; a batter therefore must not assume the bunting position until the ball is about to leave the pitcher's hand. There are three bunting positions for the body.

The traditional bunting stance calls for the batter to square around by moving the rear foot in line with the front foot so that the feet are about 12 to 18 inches apart just as the pitcher begins the delivery. *Angle* bunting has become more popular because the batter tends to pop-up less, can get into position faster and get a faster start to first base.

Figure 4.9
Stance for sacrifice bunting.

Figure 4.10
Side view of stance for sacrifice bunting.

Figure 4.11
Rear view of stance for sacrifice bunting.

Sacrifice Bunt

1. Stand near the front of the batter's box.
2. Move the rear foot in line with the front foot about 12 to 18 inches apart as the pitcher begins the delivery.
3. Face the pitcher, arms extended forward, bat held at the top of the strike zone, knees and hips slightly bent with weight on both feet.
4. Drop the bat *on top* of the ball to insure a grounded hit.

Angle Bunting

1. Stand in front of the batter's box, pivot on the balls of the feet and shift most of the weight to the front foot, bend the body forward and relax the knees, position the front feet very close to the plate and hold the head directly behind the bat.
2. Hold the bat at a 45-degree angle at all times, bring the bat head in front of the plate and face, and keep it over the plate.
3. Hold the top hand a little more than halfway up the bat with both hands together or slightly apart, hold the bat loosely with the top hand to control resistance or give when the ball hits the bat to "kill" the forward speed of the ball, and bend the elbows to keep the bat about one-half arm length away from body.

The ball is directed by the bottom hand. To place the ball down the first base line, push the bottom hand out and away from the body but maintain the 45-degree angle. To place the ball down the third base line, pull the bottom half of the bat toward the body, keeping the 45-degree angle.

Offensive Skills 27

Figure 4.12
Angle bunting with hands apart.

Figure 4.13
Angle bunting with hands together.

Figure 4.14
The grip.

Figure 4.15
Drag bunt.

Drag Bunt

1. Move your feet and arms as they normally move for a full swing.
2. Slide the top hand 6 to 8 inches up the handle just before the ball reaches the plate.
3. Stride toward first base as the ball is contacted.

Push Bunt

1. Move hands and feet as for a drag bunt.
2. Reduce the amount of give and push the ball with enough force between the fielders.

From your observation of softball games, toward which direction do the majority of the hits travel? Do you know why it is preferable to place-hit by adjusting your timing rather than your stance?

Figure 4.16
Push bunt.

Positioning the bat at the top of the strike zone insures hitting the ball downward with the bottom portion of the bat. The batter lowers the level of the bat by bending the knees and hips while keeping the arms extended. The bat should be angled downward to the left, the center, or to the right, depending on where you wish to place the bunt. Low pitches are the easiest to bunt. High, inside pitches are extremely difficult to bunt because the bat must be brought upward, resulting in a tendency to hit up, rather than down on the ball.

Fake Bunting

A fake or slap bunt is often attempted to pull the defense in toward the batter in order to help a base runner steal or to permit the batter to place-hit the ball in the defensive position vacated. Preferably, the ball should be batted just over the first or third baseman's head or into the area vacated by the second baseman or shortstop when he/she has moved to cover a base. When you are going to bluff or bunt to facilitate a base hit, deliberately move into bunting position but do not hit the ball. On the next pitch momentarily move into bunting position and then bring the bat quickly back for the backswing and swing forcefully forward at the ball. If you are faking a bunt to help a runner steal, simply move into bunting position but do not bunt the ball. This action causes the infield to draw in and forces the shortstop to move to cover second or third, depending on which base is being attempted.

Safety

Batting has two major safety hazards: being hit by the pitched ball and hitting someone with the bat. The former requires absolute alertness by the batter to avoid being hit. The use of a batting helmet is increasing to avoid injuries to the head from a pitched ball. The latter requires the batter to develop the habit of dropping the bat rather than throwing it. Spectators and other players except the team on the field should be kept at least 20 feet from home plate.

Offensive Skills

BATTING PROBLEMS AND CORRECTIONS

Problem	Causes	Corrections
No power	Grip choked	Use medium or long grip.
	Hitting off rear foot	Shift weight forward as bat swings forward.
	No wrist snap	Uncock wrist as ball is contacted.
Missing ball	Swinging too late	Use choke grip.
	Swinging too early	Use medium or long grip.
	Lack of concentration	See bat hit the ball.
Ball hit too far to batter's side	Early swing	Long or medium grip.
	Forward foot moved backward	Shorten stance and step toward the pitch.
Ball hit too far to side away from batter	Late swing	Choke or medium grip.
	Forward foot moved toward plate	Lengthen stance and step toward the pitch.
Ball is popped up	Swing is late	Swing sooner or faster.
	Swinging upward	Level swing.
	Dropping the shoulder	Keep shoulders level.
Ball is hit into ground	Chopping downward	Level swing.
Bunt goes too far	Dominant hand not giving	Relax dominant hand and recoil arms.
Bunt is popped up	Hitting high pitches	Hit only waist-high or lower pitches.
	Not pushing downward	Follow-through downward.

Practice

All practice, whether pursued individually or in a group, should be directed at achieving certain goals such as placement, power, level swing, stride and concentration.

Individual

Bat Swinging

Assume proper stance and visualize the ball coming to various corners over the plate. Attempt to swing to hit the ball.

30   *Chapter 4*

Figure 4.17
Batting tee.

Swing the bat while looking at yourself in the mirror. Check stride, position of arms and level of swing.

Swing two or three bats for a short period of time to build arm strength and thus increase the power of your swing.

Repeat the above exercises while employing bunting technique.

Batting Tee

Swing at a ball on a batting tee. If you cannot obtain one for practice, make one by attaching a 10-inch metal tube to a wooden base. Extend the tube to normal batting height by attaching a rubber radiator hose to it. The ball should be hit slightly ahead of the plate. See figure 4.17.

Adjust the tee position and adjust follow-through to practice place-hitting at various targets.

When practicing with a batting tee, try to send five successive hits to the left side of the field, five to the center, and five to the right. Can you score three out of each five? four out of five? five out of five?

Group

Group practice gives you the advantage of practicing under the watchful eye of an expert who can observe your mistakes and give you advice on how to overcome them.

Regular Pitcher

The best batting practice is against a regular pitcher. Practice swinging at balls pitched to certain target spots. Include concentrated placement, power and bunting practice.

Offensive Skills

Figure 4.18
Pepper practice.

Pitching Machine

Adjust the machine to pitch the ball at various speeds and targets.

Pepper

Two hitters stand about 15 to 20 feet in front of the group and practice hitting balls thrown or pitched by members of the group in rapid succession. Additional balls may be added. This practice is excellent for training the eyes to follow the ball. The ball should be chopped downward to hit the ball directly back to members of the group. See figure 4.18.

Evaluation

A good way to evaluate batting is to utilize a checklist to determine accuracy of form, but more importantly, the best measure is your batting average. You can figure it by dividing the total number of hits you have made by the total number of times you have been at bat. A batting average of .300 or more is considered excellent.

Baserunning

You will be able to—

1. run efficiently and swiftly to first base and to other bases after becoming a base runner, and
2. slide on close plays to avoid being tagged.

Softball games are often decided by one run. Alert, aggressive, intelligent baserunning often can make the difference between winning or losing. If you are playing on a team and have coaches at first and third bases, allow the coaches to assist you in determining your baserunning actions. Always know where you are and what the situation is relative to other base runners, number of outs, score of the game, count on the batter and throwing ability of the defensive team.

Batting Evaluation		
Name _____		Date _____
Key: 5 = Excellent; 4 = Very Good; 3 = Average; 2 = Fair; 1 = Poor		

Item	Rating	Comments
1. Ready Position	5 4 3 2 1	
2. Bat Position	5 4 3 2 1	
3. Swing	5 4 3 2 1	
4. Follow-through	5 4 3 2 1	
5. Weight transfer	5 4 3 2 1	

Figure 4.19
Batter evaluation form.

Figure 4.20
Takeoff to first base.

Running to First Base

(See figure 4.20.)

1. Push off on forward foot (left, for right-handed batters).
2. Step forward with right foot.
3. Run as fast as possible in a straight line and touch the base with either foot.
4. Do not break stride to look at the ball unless it is behind you or you have no coach.
5. Run full speed over first base if a play is expected there, pull up as soon as possible in event of an overthrow to enable advancing.
6. Curve your run to round the bag if the play is away from first base and touch the inside corner of the bag with your left foot.

Offensive Skills

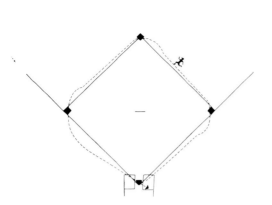

Figure 4.21
Rounding the bases.

Figure 4.22
Touching the base.

Running to Bases beyond First Base

1. Turn out to the right several feet before reaching first base by leaning to the right and taking a couple of steps at an angle away from the foul line.
2. Plan to touch the inside corner of the bag without slowing down as you change directions.
3. Touch the bag with either foot as you round the bag, but be prepared to stop if it seems unlikely that you will be able to make it to second base.
4. Straighten out run toward the next base.
5. Continue to curve out several feet before each base you intend to round.
6. Run straight to a base to which the play is to be made.
7. Touch the inside corner of the bag with your left foot and cross your right foot toward the next base. (See figure 4.22.)

Sliding

A good base runner should slide on close plays except when running from home to first base. A slide has two advantages. First, it will stop your run without causing you to lose speed; second, it will give the infielder a small target to touch if it is a tag play. There are four basic types of slides: straight-in, bent-leg, headfirst, and hook. (See figures 4.23, 4.24, and 4.25.) When planning to slide, do not slow your speed during your approach to a base.

The *straight-in slide* starts about 10 feet from the bag. Lean away from the base and lift up either leg while momentarily extending the other leg downward to the ground. This action will cause the bottom leg to skid along the ground. To prevent the spikes from catching, the skidding leg should immediately be bent at the knee and the extended leg lifted well off the ground. The arms do not come in contact with the ground.

Figure 4.23
Bent-leg slide.

Figure 4.24
Headfirst slide.

The *bent-leg slide* is executed in order to stop your speed at a base but allows you to get back on your feet immediately to proceed to another base if possible. Choose this slide if you are unsure about the accuracy of the throw or the closeness of the play. The bent-leg slide is like the straight-in slide except that it is started nearer the base and the backward fall is checked. The nonsliding leg is bent at the knee instead of extended. As soon as the skidding leg touches the base, the weight is brought forward by thrusting the arms forward, thus pulling the body up and shifting the weight to the top leg, which is bent and ready to brace your next running step with the unweighted sliding leg.

Offensive Skills 35

Figure 4.25
Hook slide.

The *headfirst* slide has increased in popularity despite its potential for upper body injury because it provides an extremely small tag area. The slide begins about 8 feet from the bag. Lean forward toward the base, extend the arms and catch your weight on the heels of the hands and chest. Keep your head up. Lean forward toward the base by dropping the head and shoulders. Push off with one leg and land on the stomach, abdomen and thighs to glide along the ground. The hands and arms should be extended toward the base. Bend the knees so that the feet do not drag along the ground. Keep the head back and hands up to avoid injuring them.

The *hook slide* is used to avoid a tag by the infielder. The sliding foot barely touches the corner of the bag away from the fielder, and the body falls away from the base. This action allows a very small part of the body to be touched by the ball. The takeoff for a hook slide may be with either foot. Again the weight is thrown backward, but both feet are bent sideways to prevent the spikes from catching. As the touching foot approaches the bag, the upper part of the body and the nonsliding leg are twisted away from the fielder. Once you make a decision to slide, never change your mind! If you change your mind, your spikes might catch the turf and could cause a leg injury.

When sliding, what must you do to prevent your spikes from catching the turf?

The Leadoff

Once you have gained a base, you of course will want to reach the next base. Until the heel of the pitcher's foot crosses the front edge of the pitcher's plate as the pitch is made, you must stay on your base. You may not lead off in 12-inch slow-pitch softball. It is important, however, that you be ready to run. A good leadoff is essential for advancing to another base, either by stealing (fast pitch only) or by advancing on a batted ball.

Figure 4.26
Conventional leadoff stance.

Figure 4.27
Rolling-start leadoff.

An effective stance is crucial to the success of a good leadoff. The left foot is placed on the inside edge of the base; the other foot may be placed either a step in front or a step behind the left foot. The latter method is used to get the body in motion before the ball leaves the pitcher's hand. A stride is taken as the pitcher's arm starts forward, but the runner must be careful not to leave the base before the ball is released. This stance should not be used in slow-pitch softball. Regardless of the method, the body faces the next base, knees are flexed and the weight is on the forward foot. Arms are bent and held free of the body, ready to generate momentum. The runner takes two or three steps, stops and returns if the ball is not hit. The body should be kept under control. When on third base, lead off in foul territory to avoid being called out for being hit with a batted ball.

Strategy

Successful baserunning requires quick and intelligent decisions. Assess the situation.

Force Out, Less Than Two Outs

—on a grounder, run as hard as possible and slide to break up a possible double play.
—on a fly ball, if you can advance, tag up until ball is caught and leave immediately for the next base.
—on a low line drive that could be caught, go halfway up the base path so that you can advance if not caught or return if it is caught.

Force Out, Two Outs

—on contact with ball, run hard to next base.
—on full count to batter, run as soon as the ball leaves the pitcher's hand.

Offensive Skills 37

Non-Force Out, Less Than Two Outs

—on second base, advance to third if ball is grounded behind you. If grounded in front of you hold up until the ball is thrown to first base and then attempt to reach third base.

—on third base, tag up on fly ball immediately and score if possible. Hold up if grounded until the ball goes through or is thrown to first base.

What are the advantages of the bent-leg slide? Hook slide?

Stealing

Stealing a base is legal only in fast-pitch softball. It enables a team to get runners into scoring position without using a sacrifice out. Furthermore, the threat of stealing often unsettles the defense and often causes errors.

A successful base stealer must be fast and alert to conditions that may enhance the success of the steal. Study the pitcher and the catcher and watch the infielders for weaknesses that may enhance the success of an attempted steal. It will help you to steal a base if the catcher has a weak throwing arm or tends to ignore your leadoff, or if the infielders seem to be slow to protect the base you seek. Regardless of these weaknesses, if a coach is not giving directions the following should be considered before attempting to steal:

1. Game score
2. Pitcher's ability
3. Number of outs
4. Ability of succeeding batters
5. Inning you are playing

If you plan to steal the next base, it is important that you do not reveal your intent before the heel of the non-pivot foot crosses the front edge of the pitcher's plate as the ball is delivered so that you will not alert the defensive team. As soon as the foot crosses the pitcher's plate, lower your body, accelerate with short, digging steps and lengthen to full stride until the base is reached. Be prepared to slide.

Delayed Steal

This is a risky play and should be attempted only by swift runners. Lead off the base as usual. If the catcher does not force you back, immediately take off at full speed for the next base as soon as he/she starts to throw the ball to the pitcher. This type of steal can be most effective if there are less than two outs and runners are on first and third bases. The runner on first runs about halfway to second and stops or slows down, deliberately tempting the catcher to throw. If the ball is thrown to second, the runner on third base breaks toward home at full speed. If the ball is not thrown to second, the first-base runner can take second base unchallenged.

38   *Chapter 4*

BASERUNNING PROBLEMS AND CORRECTIONS

Problem	Causes	Corrections
Slow start from plate or base	Striding too far on the first step	Take short, digging steps.
	Not keeping weight low	Don't look at ball; keep head down.
Sliding too early	Misjudging beginning distance	Place markers to the side of sliding area for practice.
Sliding too late	Indecision	Plan to slide and do it.

Safety

Baserunning can be one of the most dangerous aspects of softball play. You should follow these suggestions:

1. Be aware of fielders and attempt to avoid collisions.
2. Contact the corner of the base away from the baseman whenever possible to avoid bumping him.
3. Never change your mind while in the act of sliding.
4. Avoid sliding without proper protection for your legs.
5. Slide to avoid contact with the baseman.

Practice

Individual

Actual Baserunning

Practice overrunning first base; then, making the turn; then, running to first and second bases; then running from first to third; and finally, running all the way. Carry a stopwatch. Try to improve your time.

Starts

Swing bat and take off to full stride. Repeat several times. Stand on base and take off to full stride.

Sliding

Slide on a smooth surface indoors such as a gymnasium floor to a loose base in your stocking feet only. Then try grass; then use a sand pit; and finally, slide on the dirt. Wear protective clothing.

Offensive Skills 39

Group

Baserunning

Run in pairs to the various bases. Time each player's run.

Stealing

Place base runner on first base. Have the pitcher pitch and have the catcher attempt to throw the runner out.

Starts

Base runner assumes leadoff stance, leaves on signal, stops on whistle and returns.

Evaluation

Develop a checklist to evaluate starts, leadoffs and slides. Keep a record of the attempted steals, and divide the successful attempts into the total attempts to secure the percentage of successful attempts. Time each player's running speed to the various bases.

References

Craig, Susan and Johnson, Ken. *The Softball Handbook*. West Point, New York: Leisure Press, 1984, Chapters 3–7.

Drysdale, Sharon J. "A Bunting Guide." *1979–81 Softball Guide*. Washington, D.C.: National Association for Girls' and Women's Sports, American Alliance for Health, Physical Education and Recreation.

Houseworth, Steven D. and Francine V. Rivkin. *Coaching Softball Effectively*. Champaign, Illinois: Human Kinetics Press, 1985.

Johnson, Connie Peterson with Wright, Margie. *The Woman's Softball Book*. New York, New York: Leisure Press, 1984, Chapters 8–10.

Jones, Billie J. and Murray, Mary Jo. *Softball Concepts for Coaches and Teachers*. Dubuque, Iowa: Wm. C. Brown Company Publishers, 1978, Chapters 5–6.

Marcotte, Joan. "Using the Batting Tee." *1979–81 Softball Guide*. Washington, D.C., National Association for Girls' and Women's Sports, American Alliance for Health, Physical Education and Recreation.

Messler, Stephan P. and Brady, Mary Ann. "The Mechanics of Batting: A Brief Review of Current Research." *1985–87 Softball Guide*. National Association for Girls' and Women's Sports, Reston, Virginia: American Alliance for Health, Physical Education and Dance.

Wenk, Robert. *Coaching Youth Softball*. New York, New York: Leisure Press, 1984, Chapters 3–5.

Defensive Skills

5

The shortness of the base paths and the size of the ball give the offensive team an advantage. Consequently, good softball play requires good defensive play. Every player needs to possess skill in fielding ground balls, catching fly balls, and the ability to throw with speed and accuracy. In addition, knowledge of where to throw and when and how to protect a base is vital to good defensive playing ability.

Fielding

Instructional Objectives

You will be able to—

1. field ground balls and throw out a runner,
2. catch fly balls in both the infield and outfield,
3. receive throws and tag out a runner,
4. plan ahead so that cutoff plays, backing up and base covering are executed.

Catching fly balls, stopping balls hit on the ground and catching throws are the basic skills needed for good fielding. In all cases there are common principles that govern the proper fielding of the ball.

Stance

Whenever you are in a defensive position, you must be alert and ready. Figure 5.1 illustrates the proper waiting or ready position. Infielders should set with their arms barely off the ground by bending the legs and extending their arms. Outfielders should set about halfway between the infielders' ready stance and normal standing.

1. Feet are comfortably spread.
2. Body faces batter, and eyes are fixed on ball.
3. Knees and hips are bent.
4. Weight is on balls of both feet.
5. Keep the glove out in front, wide open and facing the batter.

The ready position is assumed as the ball leaves the pitcher's hand. The defensive fielders must constantly watch the batter, not the pitcher, and react immediately to batted balls; they must track the ball vigilantly.

Figure 5.1
Waiting positions.

a　　　　　　　　　　　　b　　　　　　　　　　　　c

Figure 5.2
Fielding the ball. (a) Lining up the ball. (b) Trapping the ball in the glove. (c) Moving the hands to a throwing position.

It is important that you stay relaxed throughout your fielding attempt. If the ball is hit or thrown softly, or shallow, or to the left or right, move diagonally toward it. Conversely, if it is hit or thrown sharply or deeply to the left or right, move diagonally backward. The speed of your movement depends on the exact speed of the ball and the distance it is from you.

Catching the Ball

Catching a softball requires similar basic techniques:

1. Move the body so that it is in line with the ball.
2. Watch the ball into the glove or mitt.
3. Catch the ball in the pocket of the glove or mitt.

4. Trap the ball into the glove or mitt with the throwing hand to help secure it and to allow a quick grip on the ball for the return throw.
5. Move the glove or mitt toward the body as the ball enters the pocket to absorb the impact of the ball. This is called *giving*.
6. Place the fingers of the glove or mitt upward if the ball is above your waist and downward, if below the waist.

Fly Balls

When a *fly ball* is hit, move at the crack of the bat in the direction of the ball. Run as fast as you can so that you can be there in time to wait for it, if at all possible. The speed, direction, height and effect of the wind on the ball should be determined immediately, and a judgment should be made as to about where the ball can be caught. This judgment is made as you are already on the move to that spot. The sound of the bat against the ball, as well as the visual sighting of the speed of the ball, will give you some immediate information as to where to go. If the ball is hit high, you will have a little more time to get there than if the ball is hit low. Be prepared for final adjustments while waiting for the ball to descend if a high wind is blowing. If the ball is going to come down behind you, turn to whichever side is necessary, using whatever footwork comes naturally. Look over your shoulder at the ball as you move backward and sideways for it. Try to avoid having to turn your back on the ball. Be sure you are back far enough to catch the ball, because it is easier to take a step or two forward than it is to back up. As the ball descends, get ready for the ball by standing with your legs comfortably spread, with the leg opposite to the throwing arm slightly ahead so that you are ready to throw. Try to reach about head high for the ball to save time in making the catch; and when running for the ball, have your glove out ready to catch it. Always try to be prepared to return the ball quickly. When

Figure 5.3
Judging a fly ball.

Figure 5.4
One-hand catch of fly ball.

Defensive Skills 43

Figure 5.5
Protecting against the fence.

Figure 5.6
Protecting against the sun.

Figure 5.7
Moving back to catch a fly ball.

there are base runners and if time permits, attempt to run or "loop" back a few steps behind where you plan to catch the ball so that you will be moving toward the base that you expect to be throwing to as you catch the ball. Improvements in gloves have increased the use of catching fly balls with one hand. Such a practice increases range and stability.

The presence of the fence and sun present difficult encounters for the fielder. The effects of the sun can be avoided by trying to turn the body to look away from it. Use sunglasses if possible and/or use the hand or glove to shield the sun. You can avoid running into a fence by reaching back with the non-glove hand to gauge your distance from the barrier.

Figure 5.8
Moving in to catch a fly ball.

What should you do to avoid running into a fence while fielding a ball? How can you avoid the glare of the sun while fielding a fly?

Try to catch every ball in your area unless by catching a foul you would allow a base runner to advance or score in a close game. As soon as you know you can catch the ball, warn your teammate by shouting, "I have it!" If you hear this signal from someone else before you call it, immediately move away from the ball to avoid collision with the teammate who is fielding the ball. Collisions may result in errors or serious injuries.

Ground Balls

Ground balls seldom are affected by a wind factor, but the surface of the playing field often causes the ball to bounce erratically, which causes difficulty in judging where to catch it. Just as in fielding fly balls, the decision based on the sound of the crack of the bat against the ball and the speed and direction of the ball must be made immediately so that no time is wasted in getting in the proper place to stop the ground ball. Since the batter is not out on a ground ball until the ball reaches the base he/she is attempting to reach, move quickly toward the ball. Avoid letting the ball "play you" by not moving backward on it. Shift your weight forward, pivot toward the side the ball is coming from, and run in a low position to save time in bending down for the ball at the last second. Time your run so that you can catch the ball just after it starts its bounce. This timing will avoid erratic twists and will save time. Use crossover steps when you must run a considerable distance and sidesteps when the distance is short. Crossing the legs when moving laterally will generate the needed speed to get to the ball. Sidestepping is slower but surer for reaching balls that are hit closer to you and thus will insure greater control. As the ball nears you, stop running and brace yourself by spreading your feet comfortably.

Defensive Skills 45

Figure 5.9
Fielding a ground ball.

Figure 5.10
Crossing over for a grounder.

There are six procedures that should be used for stopping ground balls. (Study figure 5.9.)

1. Place your glove-hand foot forward.
2. Bend your knees and hips low so that your hands touch the ground when hanging relaxed.
3. Move so that you are in line with the ground ball.
4. On a roller, stop the ball inside your glove-hand side foot.
5. On a hopper, pick the "best hop," preferably below waist high.
6. Watch the ball into the glove, and secure the ball with the throwing hand.

In fielding ground balls, when should you use crossover steps, and when are sliding steps preferable?

Figure 5.11
Waiting for the throw.

Figure 5.12
Catching action.

There are two difficult pickups to be made when fielding ground balls: *backhand* and *still* balls. A backhand pickup is necessary when the ball is impossible to reach in proper position on the non-glove side. In this situation, cross the glove and side foot over in front of the non-glove foot, and pivot body so that the back is toward the ball. Now reach for the ball with the glove hand while turning the glove over to smother it. Keep your eyes on the ball and your body low. As the ball enters the glove, bring the non-glove foot forward, and put the base hand into the glove to prepare for the throw. Speed is needed to field a stopped ball. Pick it up with the bare hand, watch the ball, stay down, pick it up in front of the non-glove foot and shift weight to the glove foot as you throw.

Always try to stop the ball with the glove-side foot forward and near the inside of that foot. This action allows better viewing of the ball and places the body in a good balanced position for throwing. If the ball is hit slowly, charge the ball by cutting diagonally to the right or left if necessary. If the ball is hit with great speed, move diagonally backward to the right or left. If there is not enough time to get the glove-side foot forward, try to block the ball with the body and/or field the ball off the non-glove foot. Occasionally a ground ball may bounce high, in which case the ball is taken about head high. Use two hands to field the ball if possible. Concentration, alertness and quickness are essential to good fielding of ground balls.

Thrown Balls

The same ready position is assumed for catching *thrown balls* as is used for grounders or fly balls. However, the position should not be assumed until the last moment before the ball is to be caught. This avoids warning the approaching base runners of the closeness of the play.

Defensive Skills 47

below waist   above waist

Figure 5.13
Catching position.

First, wait for the ball in a position of readiness with the feet comfortably spread, weight evenly distributed on the balls of the feet and on the hips, with knees slightly bent. Never take your eyes off the ball. If the ball comes to you below your waist, put your little fingers together and point the fingers downward; if it comes to you above your waist, put the thumbs together and point your fingers upward. This hand action permits better arm freedom and eliminates the possibility of the ball jamming the ends of your fingers. Next, as the ball enters the mitt or glove, allow your hands to retreat toward your body. This action is called "giving" and deadens the speed of the ball so that it is less likely to bound out of the glove. Simultaneously with the "give," cover the ball with your throwing hand so that the ball is trapped inside the glove. Immediately begin to grip the ball for the throw (see figure 5.13).

Why is it important to put the thumbs together and point the fingers upward when catching a ball above the waist?

FIELDING PROBLEMS AND CORRECTIONS

Problem	Causes	Corrections
Misjudging the ball	Not paying attention	Concentrate. Talk it up.
	The wind	Check wind direction and strength.
	Slow jump on ball	Move in the direction that the ball is pitched.
Late arriving	Not ready	Assume a ready stance.
	Poor start	Keep balanced.
Fumbling	Thinking about throwing	Concentrate first on catching the ball.
Bad hop on ball	Rough infield	Smooth out.
Dropping throws or flies	Not "giving"	Relax hands as ball reaches glove.

48   Chapter 5

Figure 5.14
Covering a base.

Figure 5.15
Tag at a base.

Figure 5.16
Tag for the upright runner.

Covering the Base

If the catch is a force-out play, catch the ball, touch the base and move immediately out of the way so that you are free to make another throw and are safe from being bumped by the runner. As the throw is made, decide where the ball will come. If the ball comes directly to the base, the baseman should move to the side of the base where the ball is coming. Place one foot on the base and stretch out to meet the throw with glove hand and glove-side foot.

Tag Play

(Study figure 5.15.)
If the play is a tag play away from the base, make the tag and move away. The runner may be tagged with the ball in the glove. Avoid tagging a runner with the ball in your bare hand, where it can easily be jarred loose. For a tag play at a base, straddle the bag and place your glove hand in front of the base, and let

Defensive Skills 49

Figure 5.17
Fielding and throwing.

the runner slide into it. Keep yourself balanced, weight forward, so that you can avoid being "taken out of the play" by colliding with the oncoming base runner.

Straddle the corner of the base that allows you to face the ball and the runner. If time permits, it is better to make the tag a bit up the base path but slightly off line from the runner.

A fielder must be alert and ready to judge the ball accurately and quickly, to run rapidly and catch the ball surely, and to execute the throw immediately. Fielders must watch the ball until it is firmly resting inside their glove.

Safety

Keep several things in mind when playing defense to protect against injury.

1. When waiting for a throw, keep your feet on the side of the base so they will not be stepped on.
2. Keep your throwing hand protected behind the glove or mitt.
3. When forcing out a base runner, touch the base with your foot and move quickly away to avoid a collision.
4. When fielding a fly ball or grounder where it is possible for more than one fielder to reach it, the player in the best position should call out his intentions.
5. Protect your throwing hand by fielding only with the glove hand.
6. Protect the fielded ball by immediately placing the throwing hand over the ball and gripping it so that a throw may easily be made if necessary.

Practice

Individual

Grounders

Stand several feet from a wall and throw the ball against it so that it will rebound off the wall to the floor or ground. Stop it in proper fielding position.

Fly Balls or Pop-ups

The ability to judge and catch pop-ups or fly balls can be improved by throwing a ball as high in the air as possible and then trying to catch it.

Group

Grounders

Throw or bat a grounder to each baseman, beginning with the third baseman, then the shortstop, and so on. Each fielder throws the ball to the first baseman, who throws it to the catcher. The catcher throws the ball back to first base, and the ball is then thrown to different basemen covering the bases.

Fly Balls

Throw or bat fly balls to each outfielder who then throws the ball on one bounce to the catcher or to a cutoff fielder, who relays the throw on command.

Catching Fly Balls

Work in pairs. Have one teammate or coach throw or bat fly balls. Practice catching fly balls that are hit (a) directly to you, (b) several feet over your head, (c) several feet in front of you, and (d) several feet diagonally forward, sideways ·and backwards to the right and then to the left. Work for three out of three tries before changing directions.

Reaction Footwork Drill

While facing a leader, the fielders move to positions on the field. On command they move forward, sideways, backward, utilizing proper pivoting and body positions for fielding.

Evaluation

Fielding success may be evaluated by keeping a record of your fielding average (see figure 5.18). It is computed by dividing your total putouts and assists by your total putouts, assists and errors. A fielding average of .970 or better is considered excellent.

Figure 5.18
Fielding checklist.

Figure 5.19
Grounder test.

Fielding Grounders Test[1]

Use dimensions listed in figure 5.19.

Testee fields twenty grounders thrown by the tester every five seconds into the shaded area. Each throw must strike the ground before passing line A. The testee fields the ball cleanly, tosses it aside and immediately attempts to field the next throw. Score one point for each successful pickup.

Fly Ball Test[2]

Throw twenty fly balls to a fielder in a 60-foot catching zone. The score is the number of balls caught out of two trials of ten throws each.

---

1. David K. Brace, *Skills Test Manual: Softball for Girls and Softball for Boys* (Washington, D.C.: American Association for Health, Physical Education and Recreation, 1966), pp. 30–31.
2. Ibid, pp. 32–33.

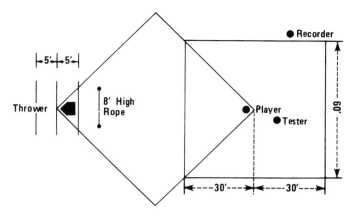

Figure 5.20
Fly ball test.

Throwing

Instructional Objectives

You will be able to—

1. throw the ball with sufficient distance and accuracy for your desired defensive position, and
2. throw the ball sidearm, if an infielder; overhand, if an outfielder; or with an overhand snap, if a catcher.

    A good portion of defensive skill depends on the ability of the fielder to throw rapidly and accurately. No matter how well you can field a ball, if you cannot throw it properly the value of your fielding will be considerably reduced.

The Grip

The ball should be gripped in one of two ways. The method you select should suit the size of your hand. If your hands are large, hold the ball between your thumb and first two fingers, with your third and fourth fingers resting against the ball as far around the bottom of the ball as you can comfortably reach. If your hands are small, modify the grip so that the third and fourth fingers are spread around the side and bottom of the ball to provide better support. If possible, the fingers should cross the seams of the ball to prevent slipping when the ball is released. Only the finger pads should touch the ball. The finger pads have the best ability to feel the ball and allow maximum joint action for whipping the throw. Do not allow any other part of the hand or palm to touch it. You should be able to see daylight between your hand and the ball. Grip the ball firmly while it is still in your glove so you can quickly and surely remove it. The glove helps to support the ball as you position your fingers.

Why should only the finger pads touch the ball as you throw?

Basic Throws

There are five basic types of throws: the overhand, the overhand snap, the sidearm, the underhand toss and the underhand pitch.

Throwing technique is basic to all throws. The major difference lies in the position of the hand and of the upper and lower arm in the forward thrust of the arm in the throw.

Overhand Throw

Only the arm position on the windup, or backswing, and the follow-through vary with the various types of throws. The basic throw for all players and the only throw used by outfielders is the overhand throw. The advantage of the overhand throw is the speed and power that can be imparted to it. The disadvantage of the overhand throw is the extra time it takes. In using the overhand throw, raise the upper arm shoulder high, lift the forearm above the head, and flex the wrist so that your hand points behind you. Lift your upper arm overhead as you move the arm forward. Make your follow-through downward. These are the steps to follow to make a good overhand throw:

1. Grip the ball firmly in the glove.
2. Shift weight backward to non-glove side foot as you bring your non-glove hand backward.
3. Cock the wrist as you momentarily point non-glove side elbow backward while it is shoulder high.
4. Move glove-side foot foward and rotate your hips toward the target as the non-glove side elbow comes forward near the head and the weight shifts to the forward foot.
5. Release the ball with a wrist snap as it passes the head.
6. Continue to let the body and arm follow-through freely and naturally.

A maximum backward stretch will develop power for your throw. The whipping action begins in the shoulder. When you release the ball, you will be off-balance unless you let your rear leg move forward to about shoulder distance from your supporting leg. If you stop the follow-through, you will lose power and accuracy.

For a long throw from the outfield, the ball is released a bit sooner than in the basic release in order to send it in a higher trajectory. The shorter the throw, the later it is released. If the throw is for a force-out play, aim it shoulder high at the receiver. If the throw is for a tag-out, it should be aimed at the base. If you must make a long throw, such as from the outfield to home plate, you can eliminate throwing the ball too high by planning to throw the ball so that it will land about 10 feet in front of the receiver. The ball can then be caught on one bounce.

What is your point of aim on a throw for a tag-out? for a force-out? for a long throw to home plate?

Figure 5.21
Throwing grips.

Figure 5.22
Throwing action.

Overhand Snap

The overhand snap throw is used primarily by the catcher and occasionally by infielders when they don't have time for a full windup. The overhand snap is executed similarly to the overhand throw, except that the windup and follow-through are shortened in order to save time. The windup ends when the ball is

Defensive Skills 55

Figure 5.23
Overhand snap.

brought about to the ear. A powerful wrist snap is important in order to gain the distance needed. The follow-through ends almost immediately after the ball is released.

Underhand Toss

The underhand toss is used on short throws that must be made quickly. The upper arm and forearm are both extended down in the backswing. The wrist extends so that the hand is pointing upward. On the forward swing, the arm comes forward with the upper arm extending downward; but as the ball is released, the upper arm extends forward. If you need to cover considerable distance, whip the forearm and wrist forcefully forward. The follow-through should be up and overhead.

Sidearm Throw

The sidearm throw is most often used by infielders to throw the ball when they are in a hurry. It is executed by extending the upper arm diagonally out and down from the shoulder and extending the forearm directly up from the elbow. As the arm is brought forward, the upper arm maintains its relative position, but the forearm is dropped down so that it is parallel with the ground. When the ball is released, the arm continues around the body sideways.

Underhand Pitch

The underhand pitch is used to deliver the ball to the batter. The details of proper pitching technique are discussed in Chapter Six.

Figure 5.24
Sidearm.

Figure 5.25
Underhand pitch.

Advanced Defensive Skills

The Preplan

Every defensive player should be thoroughly acquainted with the ability of the batter, the placement of the base runners, the placement of the defense, the score, the number of outs and the count on the batter. Develop a plan of action for all the various possibilities for a play in your area. As the ball is pitched, be ready to move and be convinced that the play will be in your area. Never hesitate. Hesitation time can make the difference between an out and a hit.

Cutoff Throws

The purpose of a cutoff throw is to put out an advancing runner but at the last second to allow for changing the play if the throw promises to be unsuccessful. The intervening fielder places herself in line with the throw and redirects it or allows it to continue to its original destination. The decision to let the throw go through or to cut it off is made with the help of a nearby noninvolved teammate who can assess the possible success of the throw. The fielder must throw the ball on a line so that it is not too high for the intervening field to catch.

It is desirable for the team to predesignate the caller for cutoff throws. Usually, catchers are in the best position to call out "come through" or "cutoff." Cutoff on throws from right field to home plate are most often made by the first baseman, from the left field by the shortstop and from center field by the second

Defensive Skills 57

Figure 5.26
Cutoff throw.

baseman. Although the pitcher may cutoff, he/she most often is used to back up the initial intended play. There are varying opinions concerning who should take the cutoff throw.

When should the intervening fielder catch a cutoff throw play?

Safety

Follow these procedures to protect against injury.

1. Warm up your arm before attempting difficult throws.
2. Throw the ball to basemen on the side opposite from where the base runner is expected.
3. The infielder should bend down to avoid being struck by a thrown ball intended for a player beyond him.

THROWING PROBLEMS AND CORRECTIONS

Problem	Causes	Corrections
Ball Misses Target		
Right or high	Releasing ball too soon	Snap wrist. Hold off the release a bit longer.
	Off-balance	Stress shifting weight forward and pivot.
Left or low	Releasing too late	Let go of ball sooner.
Ball Is Short of Target	Weak throwing arm	Change to less demanding position.
		Strengthen throwing arm through weight training.

Figure 5.27
Throwing practice.

Practice

Individual

Throw against a Wall

Throw a ball against a target on the wall. The ball will rebound, and if you stand close enough, you will be able to catch it on the rebound.

Throwing to Bases

Throwing to bases can be practiced by standing near a corner of a large room and throwing the ball against one wall, catching it and throwing it at the wall to your right or left.

Throwing from the Outfield

Stand in outfield position with several balls. Place a target in the infield, such as a tire or a cone, and attempt to hit it.

Throwing for Distance

After warming up your arm by practice throwing, progressively increase the distance that the ball can be thrown. Mark that distance. During each practice attempt to exceed that distance.

Group

Back and Forth

Work in pairs, facing each other. The receiver sets a target for the thrower. Winner is first player to reach 20.

Defensive Skills 59

	Throwing Evaluation	

Name _____ Date _____

Key: 5 = Excellent; 4 = Very Good; 3 = Average; 2 = Fair; 1 = Poor

Item	Rating	Comments
1. Grip	5 4 3 2 1	
2. Backward motion	5 4 3 2 1	
3. Forward motion	5 4 3 2 1	
4. Wrist snap	5 4 3 2 1	
5. Follow-through	5 4 3 2 1	

Figure 5.28
Throwing evaluation.

Three in a Line

Work in threes in a straight line. The end player with the ball throws it to the target set by the middle player who pivots after catching the ball and throws it to the opposite end player's target. Repeat going backward. Score for successful target throws may be kept. Repeat practices suggested for fielding except that the quality of the throw should be stressed.

Evaluation

There are several reliable and valid skills tests for throwing described in physical education measurement and evaluation texts. Accuracy and distance are the variables most often measured.

Throw for Distance

From a 6-foot approach area, take three tries at throwing for distance. Measure the best throw to the nearest foot.

Repeated Throwing

Throw the ball repeatedly against a wall from behind a line 15 feet from the wall. The ball must hit above a 7½-foot line. The score is the number of hits against the wall in thirty seconds. The best of six tries is counted.

The correct technique when performing softball skills may be evaluated by using a criterion checklist. Figure 5.28 is a sample of such a checklist for evaluating throwing.

References

Brace, David K. *Skills Test Manual: Softball for Girls and Softball for Boys.* Washington, D.C.: American Association for Health, Physical Education, and Recreation, 1966.

Craig, Susan and Johnson, Ken. *The Softball Book.* West Point, New York: Leisure Press, 1985, Chapters 8 and 11.

Houseworth, Steven D. and Rivkin, Francine V. *Coaching Softball Effectively.* Champaign, Illinois: Human Kinetics Press, 1985, Part II.

Johnson, Connie Peterson with Wright, Margie. *The Woman's Softball Book.* New York, New York: Leisure Press, 1984, Chapters 4, 5, and 6.

Walker, June. "Selected Outfield Techniques." *1985–87 Softball Guide.* Reston, Virginia: National Association for Girls' and Women's Sports of the American Alliance for Health, Physical Education, Recreation and Dance, pp. 17–20.

Wenk, Robert. *Coaching Youth Softball.* New York, New York: Leisure Press, 1984, Chapter 2.

Defensive Skills 61

Defensive Position Play

6

Fielding and catching are the fundamental defensive measures. The defensive team prevents runs from scoring by using these skills; however, each position requires its special application. All softball players should understand the basic requirements of each position in order to work together as a team.

THE PITCHER

Instructional Objectives

You will be able to—

1. pitch with accuracy in fast- or slow-pitch softball and with considerable speed in fast-pitch softball to deter successful hitting, and
2. field the ball and throw out the batter or other base runners.

The pitcher is crucial to success in fast-pitch softball. The initiation of activity begins with the pitcher, and probably 75 percent of winning in fast-pitch softball will depend upon pitching. Strength and stamina are important attributes for a pitcher. In addition, excellent physique, energy, alertness, wisdom and courage are needed. The most important requirement in either fast- or slow-pitch play, however, is accuracy or control. The pitcher must have the ability to pitch the ball consistently over the plate and in the strike zone. In fast-pitch softball, the objective is to make it impossible for the batter to hit the ball. Thus speed and deception are needed on each pitch. In slow-pitch softball, however, only accuracy is required, since the objective is to get the batter out after he has hit the ball.

Fast-pitch Pitching

Concentrated practice is necessary in order to develop and control the variety of pitches necessary. Most fast-pitch pitchers use a windmill or a slingshot type of delivery. Windups have two purposes: (1) to deceive the batter and (2) to obtain full power from your entire body to add force to the pitch. Develop the windup and delivery that suits you best. There is a variety of pitches: fastball, change of pace, drop, curves and a rise, or upshoot, pitch. Start your pitch by standing with your pivot foot, which is your glove-side foot, on the pitcher's plate and the non-pivot foot on or behind the pitcher's plate. Both feet must be on the ground within

63

RULES GOVERNING PITCHING

Action	Fast Pitch	Slow Pitch
Delivery	Underhand	Same.
Feet	The pivot foot must be in contact with pitching plate	Only one foot must be on the plate.
Step	One step may be taken toward the batter as ball is delivered	Same.
Speed	Any amount permitted	Moderate speed with a perceptible arc, not over 10 feet.
Strike Zone	Over the plate and between batter's armpits and the tops of his knees	Over the plate and no higher than the batter's shoulders or lower than his knees.
Windup	Only one motion toward the batter is legal	Same except in 16-inch play where two hesitations are permitted.

the 24-inch length of the pitcher's plate. Face the batter; your shoulders must be in line with first and third bases, and the ball shall be held in one hand. Your feet should be approximately 12 inches apart. Only from this position can you take the signal from the catcher. After assuming this "ready" position you may hold the ball in both hands for not less than one second or more than ten seconds before releasing it toward the batter.

Deliveries

The ball is delivered to the plate in predominately three ways: the windmill, sling-shot and the straight pitch.

Windmill

The *windmill delivery* makes a complete circle from straight up overhead to behind your body and then downward and out toward the batter. It is used by most advanced-level pitchers in fast-pitch softball because it generates the most momentum for speed. Start the delivery with both arms moving forward and upward, reaching out without stretching. Shift your weight to the foot on the

64   *Chapter 6*

pitching-arm side. As you take the ball from the glove, extend the upper arm diagonally outward from the shoulder and the forearm diagonally inward toward the body. As the hand reaches head-high, begin to lift the opposite foot off the rubber and forward in order to keep your balance. The arm is completely extended when it is dropped behind the body from head-high. You will gain momentum as you move into your downward swing. The non-pivot foot completes its step toward the plate in order to brace your body for the forward action and release of the ball. The pitching arm is thrust forward by pushing with the pivot foot against the rubber and then transferring this weight forward. Start the forward motion with your body rotating forward, the arm swung downward and forward, parallel with the lateral line of the body. Bring your body weight forward as you take a natural step toward the batter on the foot opposite the pitching arm. When the extended arm is about even with the side of the body just before the ball is released, snap your wrist forward and roll the ball off your fingertips to add power and spin to the pitch. After the ball leaves your hand, the arm continues to follow through, up and overhead with the arm completely extended.

Slingshot

The *slingshot* usually provides more control but with slightly less speed and it is more often used in less advanced play. Start your backswing by moving both hands forward toward the batter until your arms are comfortably extended straight out in front about waist high. When this point is reached, bring your throwing arm down and back along the hip line and up behind the body as far as it can comfortably extend. At the top of the backswing, cock your wrist by extending as far back as possible. The upper arm and forearm are diagonally upward, and the body is rotated almost a quarter turn toward the pitching-arm side. Your follow-through is similar to the windmill delivery. The foot on the pitching-arm side is brought up next to the forward foot in a fairly wide stance with the knees and hips relaxed. This position permits maximum balance after release of the ball and also puts you in a ready fielding position.

Straight Pitch

The *straight pitch* is a control pitch and is similar to the slingshot but the backswing is less. It is most often used in slow-pitch softball. The forward motion, release and follow-through are similar to the other deliveries.

As you develop your speed and control, try to release your fast pitch so that it will "break" by curving, rising, or dropping. Do not attempt to toss or pull the arm, but rather swing the arm freely and powerfully on your delivery.

Note that the difference between the windmill and slingshot deliveries is in the initial action of the pitching arm; that is, up, over, down and forward for the windmill, and back, up, down and forward for the slingshot delivery.

Defensive Position Play   65

Figure 6.1
Slingshot pitch.

Regardless of which delivery you use, the following elements are important to your pitching motion:

1. Cock the wrists on the backswing and snap them on the release.
2. Maintain balance on the forward swing by lifting the non-pivot foot as you stride forward.
3. Brush the hip at the point of release.
4. Develop a consistent stride.
5. Drive off the rubber with the non-pivot foot for power.

Which type of pitch is used most often by advanced-level pitchers in fast-pitch softball? Which type of pitch is most customary in slow-pitch games?

Figure 6.2
Pitching windups.

Types of Pitches

Once you have developed control and speed, you should learn other types of pitches. These pitches cause the ball to drop, to curve, to rise and to change speeds in order to make it more difficult for the batter to hit the ball. Regardless of the type of pitch, the pitching action should be similar so that the batter does not know what kind of a pitch to expect.

For the *straight fast pitch* and the *slingshot delivery* grip the ball as for any other throw except that the hand is under the ball. Again, as for other throws, use either your entire hand or the tripod grip. Be sure your finger pads cross the seams of the ball.

A *curveball* makes the ball spin either toward or away from the batter. To pitch a curveball, grip the ball as for the fastball, but as it is released, snap the wrist to the left or to the right to cause the ball to roll off the inside or outside of the hand. The direction of the snap depends on the direction you wish the ball to curve. Snap the wrist to the left to make the ball curve left and to the right to make it curve right. The *drop* makes the ball curve or break sharply downward. Use the same grip and delivery as for the fastball, but at the instant of the release, lift your thumb off the ball first, and then snap your first two fingers sharply upward. This action gives the ball more forward spin so that it will curve downward, or drop.

The grip for the *rise* or *upshoot pitch* differs in that the ball is held with the fingers on top of the ball with the thumb underneath. As you release the ball, the wrist is extended or snapped upward, and the thumb pushes forward against the ball. This action imparts a backspin that should make the ball rise as it nears home plate. The effectiveness of these pitches will increase as you learn to add speed to the pitch. The *change-of-pace pitch* slows down the pitch and tends to

Figure 6.3
Fast-pitch foot position.

Figure 6.4
Pitching grips and releases.

throw off the timing of the batter. There are many grips for the change-of-pace pitch. The ball may be held in the palm of the hand with the fingers held loosely on the ball. It may be held by the knuckles or by digging your fingernails into it. Your pitching motion is again the same, but at the release the hand is opened with a snap of all four fingers, and the thumb merely extends forward. The ball must be released with equal pressure all around the ball so that no spin is imparted to it. The absence of spin will cause the ball to float or sail toward the batter. Controlling these various pitches and the development of speed will give you what is called "stuff." Concentrate first on pitching with as much speed and spin as you can accurately control.

What is the effect on a pitched ball of a wrist snap to the left on the release?

Slow-pitch Pitching

Since the ball must travel through an arc of at least 6 and no more than 12 feet, many pitchers will try to control the ball so that it reaches the maximum height close to the batter. The ball will descend as it crosses the plate and will be even with his or her back shoulder. This type of pitch often results in a pop-up. The slow-pitch pitcher should try to pitch to the desired corners of the plate and vary the height of the arc of the pitched ball. It is legal and desirable to place spins on the ball: forward, backward, or sideward.

Since only one foot must be in contact with the pitching plate, be sure that the supporting foot is on the front edge of the plate so that when your stride is taken, your body can be as close to the target as possible at the instant of release.

Using a wall target, practice fast pitches to each corner of the strike zone. Can you achieve a 50-percent accuracy score? 75 percent? Try the same practice with a slow-pitch delivery.

Defensive Responsibilities

Pitchers have many defensive responsibilities. You must be able to field bunts, check runners on base, cover bases and back up throws.

After a Pitch

Receive the ball from the catcher in front of the rubber. If there is a base runner, check the runner back and be sure you are in the pitcher's circle. Walk behind the pitcher's rubber while facing second base. Turn toward the batter and assume the correct pitching position. Envision a strike on every pitch.

Bunts

In advanced play, most bunts are fielded by the first and third basemen because they move in very close to the plate. However, particular defense will necessitate your fielding bunts. Use the fielding techniques described for infielders.

Covering

Whenever the catcher leaves the plate and a runner can score, you must cover the plate. Don't block the plate. Give the runner the outside of the plate and tag with the ball in the glove.

Backing

Usually the pitcher will back up third base. Move 20 feet behind the base on a hit to the outfield when a play is anticipated.

Defensive Position Play 69

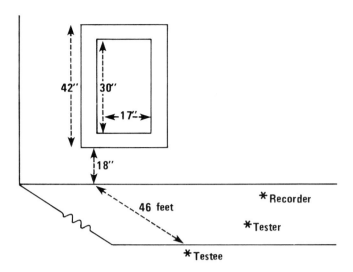

Figure 6.5
Accuracy test.

Cutoff Plays

Move approximately 20 feet in front of the plate to the side that the throw is expected. Raise both arms overhead. The catcher will call for the cutoff and where to throw the ball. If no directions are given, allow the ball to go through to the catcher.

Safety

Pitching is demanding, and it can be a dangerous position.

1. Be alert and balanced after delivering the ball to avoid being hit by sharply batted balls.
2. Be sure that the pitching plate and soil around the pitching area are firm to prevent slipping.

Practice

Individual

Mimetic Pitching

For about ten minutes daily practice your pitching form without using a ball. Assume stance, concentration, and take your windup, delivery and follow-through.

PITCHING PROBLEMS AND CORRECTIONS

Problem	Causes	Corrections
Ball too high or far from batter	Release too late or stride too short	Release sooner. Practice consistent striding by marking desired spot.
Ball too low or close to batter	Release too soon or stride too long	Release later. Practice consistent stride.
Insufficient speed	Incorrect delivery action	Increase leverage by rotating spine and hip on throwing side away from batter. Stride as arm moves forward. Move arm forward as fast as possible. Snap the wrist on release.
Loss of balance	Incorrect stride and weight shift	Practice stride. Bring pitching-side foot up parallel with supporting foot after release of the ball.
	Incorrect stance	Feet shoulder-width apart.

Evaluation

Win-Loss Record

Compile the total wins and losses.

Earned Run Record

Compute the Earned Run Average (ERA) by adding all earned runs scored against the pitcher as a result of base runners getting on base other than by errors and by adding all the innings pitched. Multiply the earned runs by seven and divide by the innings pitched. The formula is:

$$\frac{\text{ER (earned runs)} \times 7 \text{ (innings in a game)}}{\text{IP (total innings pitched)}}$$

Accuracy Test

Place a target on the wall as per figure 6.5. Fifteen legal pitches are permitted. Pitched balls striking within or on the line marking the inner rectangle count two points. Balls hitting the outer rectangle count one point. The score is the sum of points made.

What are the backing and covering responsibilities of the pitcher?

Defensive Position Play   71

Target Practice

Construct the strike zone on the wall or a piece of carpet hung in front of a wall. Take a basket of balls and pitch to planned areas on the target.

Speed

Increase speed as accuracy develops. Both should be practiced together. Try to pitch as fast as possible with accuracy.

Leg Strength

Run several times around the field daily to increase leg strength and overall physical endurance.

Group

Batting Practice

Pitch batting practice as a means of becoming accustomed to the individual batter's position and relation to the strike zone.

Observed Practice

Have someone with a checklist of the essential pitching fundamentals check out adherence to form.

The Catcher

You will be able to—

1. catch the balls thrown by the pitcher,
2. give reliable and accurate targets for the pitcher,
3. decide the pitch needed and signal the pitcher,
4. field the ball and throw out base runners,
5. direct the infield on where the play should be made on a bunt.

The Catcher

The catcher is an important defensive position in fast-pitch softball since base runners can steal bases and advance on wild pitches and passed balls. In slow pitch, the catcher may be one of the weakest fielding players because of the following differences:

1. bunting or stealing is not allowed,
2. the ball is dead after each called ball or strike, and
3. the slow arching pitch is not as dangerous as a fast straight pitch.

The catcher is the sparkplug of the team. This player not only catches the pitches but also is in the best position to direct team defensive play. The catcher should be agile, alert, strong in the legs and able to react quickly, and should be a natural leader with a competitive spirit and the ability to think quickly, decisively and logically. A strong throwing arm is essential. The catcher is responsible for giving the pitcher advice on the type of pitch and the target for the pitch, catching pop-ups, throwing out runners attempting to steal, fielding bunts, protecting home plate, and backing up play at first or third base. The rules require that the catcher be in the catcher's box to receive the pitch, not interfere with the batter's attempt to swing at the ball, and wear a mask to protect the face.

Stance

The signal and the target for the pitch are given by the catcher when in a squat position. The squat position is assumed by bending the hips, knees and ankles so that the body is as low as possible without resting the buttock on the ankles or the ground. Weight is on the toes, and knees are comfortably spread outward. At this point fast-pitch catchers choose one of two stances. Some "stand up," whereas others continue to "sit down," as illustrated in figures 6.6 and 6.7. The sit-down catcher stays on his or her haunches for the target. As the ball is pitched, the catcher rises on his or her toes into a crouch and thus is ready to meet the pitch, pivot, throw, or field. The stand-up catcher's stance is a bit more popular. Stand with knees bent and legs wide apart with the left foot ahead of the right. If the catcher is tall, this position is awkward and requires a great deal of bending. In general, the catcher's stance often depends upon the catcher's preference, ability, type of pitch and the baserunning situation.

Figure 6.6
Catcher stand-up stance.

Figure 6.7
Catcher sit-down stance.

Figure 6.8
Slow-pitch stance.

The slow-pitch catching stance usually begins about one-half a bat length further away from the plate than the fast-pitch stance. Since the ball is arching downward, the glove or mitt is held out for the target but then lowered about shin high to catch the ball before or after it bounces. (See figure 6.8.)

Signals

The catcher and pitcher should agree on signals for the pitch. The catcher gives signals by extending the fingers of the throwing hand against the inside of his/her thigh when down in a squat position. Effort must be made to hide the signal from the offensive team. The pitcher has the prerogative of refusing the signaled pitch if he/she doesn't agree with it.

Target

After the signal is accepted, give the pitcher the target for the pitch by holding your mitt at the desired spot. As you hold your mitt up for the target clench the throwing hand in a loose fist to protect the fingers from the ball. Continue to hold the mitt on the target as the pitcher starts to pitch. When the ball leaves the pitcher's hand move up to a semistanding position with your feet spread diagonally outward approximately 3 feet apart. The change of position allows greater freedom of movement to catch the ball, to field it, or to throw out a runner. If the pitch should come low into the dirt, drop your left leg down parallel with the ground to block the ball. When the ball reaches your glove or mitt, absorb the force of the pitch by "relaxing" your arms into your waist.

Avoid giving a target in the middle of the strike zone. Keep the target steady until the ball leaves the pitcher's hand. The pitcher and catcher should study the

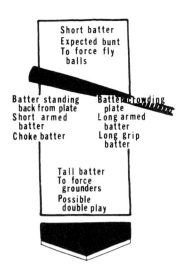

Figure 6.9
Pitching area for strike zones.

batter and organize a strategy. The pitcher should throw balls that the batter finds difficult to hit. The ball should be pitched over the inside corner of the plate to batters who stand close to the plate, and over the outside corner of the plate to batters who stand far away from the plate. If the batter crouches, pitch the ball high. If the batter stands erect, pitch low balls. Change the pace of your delivery to power hitters and pitch fastballs to weak hitters. If the batter strides toward the pitch as he/she swings, pitch the ball inside. If the stride is away, aim your pitch to the outside corner of the plate. When the batter takes a long stride into the pitch, pitch high balls; conversely, if the batter takes a short stride, pitch low balls.

If a weak batter stands erect and away from the plate, what kind of pitch is recommended?

The catcher must adjust his/her target and the type of pitch when there are base runners. With less than two outs and runners on base, the pitcher should pitch low and inside to force the batter to hit the ball into the ground for a double play or to prevent the batter from hitting the ball behind the runner on a hit-and-run play. If a bunt is expected, the pitch should be kept high because these pitches are often popped-up.

Pitching patterns depend on the pitcher's control. Every pitcher must aim at a target, however, and the target should be a most effective one for that batter at that particular time and in that particular situation.

Throwing

The preparation for throwing must be accomplished quickly. The catcher uses a snap throw to the pitcher and, if strong enough, a snap throw to throw out runners attempting to steal and to field a bunt. With runners on base, the catcher should constantly try to reduce their leadoff by walking out in front of the plate and threatening to throw to the base or by simply walking them back to base. An occasional snap throw to the base may catch a base runner too far off to get back safely.

A snap throw begins from behind the ear and is thrown overhand with a snap of the wrist. The feet must be shuffled from the squat or stand-up stance so that the nonthrowing-side hip and foot are moving toward the intended target. Do not straighten up completely nor move in front of the plate. The throw should be free of spin and aimed at the fielder's knees on the side of the anticipated play. Do not wait for the infielder to cover the base.

Fielding Responsibilities

Catchers must catch pop flies, field bunts, retrieve passed balls, wild pitches, back up first base, cover home plate, pick off runners and often direct cutoff throws. Immediately flip off the mask when you must assume a fielding responsibility.

Catching Pop Flies

Infielders should be allowed to catch pop flies if they can easily reach them. If the ball is behind you, you should turn your back to the infield and run for it. Catch the ball over your head with both hands.

The Bunt

Move with the batter, stay low, pick up the ball with your throwing hand. If the ball is toward first base, field the ball with the dominant foot forward to avoid any extra step. If the ball is down the third base side, run in a semicircle so the ball is picked up while facing first base.

Retrieving Wild Passed and Pitched Balls

No retrieval is necessary if there are no runners on base. Move immediately to retrieve the ball if there are base runners, field it and immediately turn to deter the runner from advancing or to attempt to putout.

Backing Up First Base

If there are no runners in potential scoring positions, the catcher should back up all throws to first base. Move diagonally away from the base line and toward first base as soon as a ground ball is hit.

Covering Home Plate

Await the throw in front of home plate, show the base runner only a small part of the outside corner of the plate, catch the ball, turn outside and tag the runner. If the runner is sliding, drop your right knee, turn left and put the glove low and let the runner slide into it. Blocking the plate is dangerous but is often done in advanced play.

76 *Chapter 6*

Figure 6.10
Awareness needed.

Figure 6.11
First baseman put-out position.

Picking Off

When you see that a runner is too far from the base immediately throw the ball to the covering baseman. Since you face the entire defense, you serve as the defensive leader. The catcher calls out who is to field bunts, pop-ups and short fly balls. Team spirit and hustle are encouraged and maintained by your example. If the pitcher gets upset, develops some pitching flaw, or begins to pitch too fast, the catcher should walk out to the pitcher to talk, encourage and in general try to settle the pitcher down.

Cutoff Plays

You are usually responsible for calling the play for a cutoff. Call "cut" and identify the base to which the ball is to be thrown. Give no directions if the ball is to continue on course.

Infielders

You will be able to—

1. catch balls thrown by teammates to put out base runners,
2. field batted and thrown balls,
3. cover and back up assigned bases.

Playing the infield requires specific physical ability and skill for each position. However, all infielders, including the pitcher and the catcher, must constantly be aware of the immediate situation such as (1) number of outs, (2) count on the batter, and (3) position of the base runners. With this information, you must think through what action you will need to play your position before each pitch. This process is fostered through constant communication with other infielders.

First Baseman

The first baseman is involved in almost every play. Agility and height are helpful physical attributes for this position. Throwing to other bases is easier for left-handed players. The first baseman plays about 6 feet toward second base and two

Figure 6.12
Double play with second baseman.

Figure 6.13
Force-out and relay throw.

to three steps in front of the base, one third or halfway to the plate, if the batter is fast or a sacrifice is in order to protect against a bunt. When two strikes have been called, you can move back four or five steps since a bunt is less likely. You receive all kinds of throws. Nimble footwork is essential. To cover the base for a putout, the first baseman stands in the usual ready position, facing the throw. If the ball comes straight to you, step toward the ball with the foot on the mitt side and touch the bag with the opposite foot. Reach for the ball to save time. If the ball comes wide of the mitt side, step to that side, and touch the bag with the same foot as for the straight-in throw. If the ball comes wide to the non-mitt side, reach across with the mitt to catch it and touch the base with the foot opposite the mitt side. On a pick-off play when the catcher throws the ball to try to put out the runner, if time permits, straddle the bag with your feet facing second base and rotate the upper part of your body toward the throw. When you catch the ball, swing the mitt down on the bag.

Can you throw accurate sidearm from first to third or third to first base five times in succession?

Figure 6.14
Backing up bases.

Figure 6.15
Trapping a runner.

Second Baseman

The second baseman plays about 15 feet toward first base from second base and about 10 feet behind the base line. Your job is to catch any fly balls or field any grounders in this territory. Since most of the second baseman's throws will go to first base or to the shortstop covering second base, a strong throwing arm is not necessary. However, agility in covering the base and ability to throw the ball quickly aids the second baseman in making double plays. When you are the middleman for a double play at second base, you run so that you will catch the ball as you step on the base with your left foot. After catching the ball, you take one more step with your right foot to leave the base, then pivot on the right foot, and step forward with the left foot as you throw to first base. The second baseman must be alert to receive throws from the catcher on attempted steals and on bunt plays to cover first base.

Shortstop

This very demanding position requires agility, speed and a good throwing arm. The shortstop plays about halfway between third and second base and about 10 to 12 feet behind the base line. As a shortstop you must be quick, agile, able to throw off-balance and to run rapidly. When you are the pivot man on a double play, you usually run directly to the base, reaching it in time to receive the throw, tag the base, and get rid of the ball before the base runner can break up the play. If the throw is from the second baseman, step past the bag with the left foot, drag the right foot across the bag and throw. If the throw is from the first baseman, the ball should come to the front side of the bag. In this situation, come to a quick stop, touch the base with the left foot and then throw the ball.

Defensive Position Play 79

Third Baseman

Third base is called the "hot corner" because most batters are right-handed and tend to "pull" their hits toward third base. Therefore, as a third baseman, you must be able to field and throw in a rapid, smooth sequence. The position of the third baseman in fast pitch varies according to the situation. You will be constantly changing your position. Because the bunt is so prevalent in advanced play, you will play sometimes halfway to home plate. Normally, you will play about 15 feet from third base when a bunt is expected and about 5 to 10 feet in front of third base when a bunt is not expected. Play close enough to the line so that a ball down the line could be reached with one stride. These distances will vary with the speed of the pitch and the side from which the batter bunts. You will field all ground balls and pop flies hit in your area and cover third base on all putout plays. In slow pitch the third baseman may always play back since bunting is illegal.

When playing fast pitch where should the third baseman play against good bunting teams? after two strikes?

Infielder Defensive Responsibilities

Infielders have a variety of duties to perform and their execution vary depending upon the situation relative to the score, position of base runners and placement of the batted ball. These duties are backing up and covering bases, cutting off throws and tagging out runners on a trap play.

Backing Up Bases

Every defensive player has a responsibility to back up plays in his/her area. The purpose of backing up is to prevent the taking of an additional base because of an error. The first baseman occasionally backs up home.

Covering

Each baseman is responsible for protecting his/her base. Be ready at all times to catch a throw to your base to put out a runner. However, occasionally you will be forced to field a ball while another runner is advancing to your base. In this case, the nearest available defensive player should be prepared to run to your base and take the thrown ball to put out the runner. The second baseman covers first base if the first baseman is forced to field a batted ball. In this situation, the shortstop automatically moves to second base to cover the base. If the shortstop is fielding a ball and a play is to be made to second base, the second baseman covers the base. If the third baseman is fielding the ball, the shortstop will cover third base. These covering maneuvers can often be anticipated, but when they cannot, an advanced player moves instinctively to protect the base near him/her.

Trapping a Runner

When a base runner is caught between two bases, he/she is referred to as being trapped. In this situation defensive players close in on the runner from either side, throwing the ball to the player toward whom the runner is moving. In the meantime, other players back up the throw to protect against an overthrown ball or to tag out the runner if he/she should elude the trap. It is a good technique to fake a throw and then move toward the runner with the ball. Always chase the runner back to the base they came from. Rundown fielders should position themselves slightly to the side of the base to avoid throwing into the runner.

In the meantime, the first defensive player runs at the base runner as the second defensive player positions himself/herself inside the base line just in front of the base. The first option is to be able to outrun the base runner and tag him/her out. If this is not possible, the ball should be thrown to the second defensive player to tag out the runner. This can only be accomplished if the base runner is forced to retreat at such speed that he/she cannot reverse directions.

Cutoff Plays

The pitcher may act to cutoff throws and redirect the ball if the catcher directs such action. Occasionally, the outfielder may not be able to throw on a line from where the ball is retrieved or caught. In this situation, the closest infielder must be alert to be in position to raise his/her arms in a "U" to serve as a cutoff target. Redirect the ball as directed by the catcher.

INFIELDING PROBLEMS AND CORRECTIONS

Problems	Causes	Corrections
Throw too late for a putout	Not charging the ball	Come to meet the ball.
	Taking too long to release the ball	Practice throwing from a semistanding position.
	Weak arm	Play a position needing less arm strength.
Failure to cover the base	Not thinking ahead	Infielders must communicate.
Failure to back up a play	Lack of concentration	Practice and reminders.

Practice

Individual

Mimetic Footwork

Assume ready fielding position and practice moving forward, backward and sideways to field the ball and then to move over to the base to cover.

Pivot and Throw

Place a base about 10 feet from the wall. Position yourself the usual playing distance from the base. Place a ball on the floor at that point; then, pick it up, run to the base and throw the ball against the wall.

Pop-ups

Throw a ball vertically at differing heights. Practice trying to catch the ball.

Group

Infield Practice

Throw or hit the ball from the batter's position to each infielder. The infielder fields the ball and throws to first base. The ball is then thrown to the catcher, catcher to third baseman, to second baseman, to first baseman and then back to the catcher. The catcher flips the ball to the hitter or thrower who repeats the action to each infielder. The initial throw after fielding the ball may be made to other bases.

Trapping the Runners

Place a base runner between two infielders. The base runner attempts to return or advance to a base before being put out. Fielders practice throwing the ball and chasing the runner to make the putout. Add the various backup and covering assignments of the remaining infielders.

Double Play

Place a runner on first base and a base runner at home plate. A ball is thrown or batted to an infielder, who attempts to complete the double play. (Sliding can be practiced by the runner approaching second base.)

Evaluation

Fielding Record

Keep a record of the attempted putouts and assists and the successful putouts and assists. To determine an average, divide the number of successes by the number of attempts.

$$\frac{\text{Successes}}{\text{Attempts}} = \text{Average of Fielding Success.}$$

Rating Chart

Ask an observer to evaluate your fielding performance on the chart on page 83.

Defensive Evaluation		

Name _____ Position _____

Key: 5 = Excellent, 4 = Very Good, 3 = Average, 2 = Fair, 1 = Poor

Item	Rating	Comments
1. Ready position	5 4 3 2 1	
2. Fielding position	5 4 3 2 1	
3. Throwing	5 4 3 2 1	
4. Covering	5 4 3 2 1	
5. Tagging	5 4 3 2 1	
6. Backing bases	5 4 3 2 1	

Figure 6.16
Outfielder evaluation form.

Outfielders

You will be able to—

1. catch a fly ball hit into your assigned area,
2. throw the ball to the proper infielder to force out or to contain the actions of the base runner.
3. field ground balls,
4. back up other outfielders making a play.

An outfielder must be a good runner and possess a strong throwing arm. The distance in or out that an outfielder plays depends on several factors: the wind, the batter's ability, the score, the inning and the location of base runners. In addition, the basic position is varied by moving to your right for left-handed hitters and to your left for right-handed hitters. The movement is increased in either direction for pull hitters.

Can you describe several safety precautions that should be taken to avoid injuries in throwing or catching balls?

An outfielder must learn to judge the ball immediately, run rapidly to catch the ball, and return the throw as quickly as possible. In addition to fielding the ball, outfielders back up plays at the various bases in their areas, as well as for the outfielders nearest to them. Outfielders must be aware of base runners as well as the number of outs. The outfielder must decide as the ball is caught whether he/she can throw out a base runner. If a putout is possible, he/she will throw the ball on a line directly to the base. If he/she cannot throw that far on a direct

Defensive Position Play 83

Figure 6.17
Relay throw.

line, he/she will throw the ball so that it will land a few feet in front of the base and hop into the infielder's glove. If it is not possible to gain a putout, the outfielder will return the ball one base ahead of the runner closest to home plate. Making unnecessary throws is always avoided. When the ball is hit deep and the throw is too long to reach its destination on one hop, throw to the second baseman or shortstop, who will relay the throw. The glare of the sun or field lights can sometimes hamper the vision of outfielders. Outfielders wear sunglasses, burnt cork, or shield their eyes from glare. It is the outfielder's responsibility to be aware of the wind direction and velocity, as well as the usual habits of the batter, and to adjust his or her position in the outfield accordingly. Short fly balls falling between the infield and outfield are usually the responsibility of the outfielders, since it is easier to move forward than backward. Outfielders must call out their intentions on these plays. It is imperative that outfielders communicate to each other whenever the ball is hit in areas that overlap.

Can you throw five overhead throws from left field to home plate with one bounce? without a bounce?

Center Fielder

The center fielder plays behind second base and is the fastest and most aggressive player in the outfield. As the center fielder, you are the leader of the outfield. Priority is given to you to field all balls to either the left or right. It is your responsibility to direct the proper playing positions of the other outfielders. The center fielder directs where the throw is to be made from the outfield. You will back up the other outfielders and the second baseman. When the ball is hit between two outfielders, the center fielder cuts over for the ball, and the other outfielders cut behind him to back up the play as noted in figure 6.18.

Left Fielder

The left fielder plays in the outfield between the third baseman and the shortstop, and backs up the center fielder and the third baseman when necessary. Usually the left fielder will play a bit closer to the foul line for right-handed hitters and a bit closer to center field for left-handed hitters. In addition, the left fielder backs up all throws made from the right side of the field.

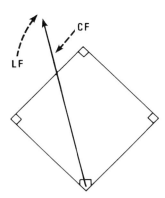

Figure 6.18
Ball hit between outfielders.

Right Fielder

The right fielder plays between first and second base, and backs up the center fielder and the first baseman when necessary. Usually the right fielder plays a bit closer to the foul line for left-handed pull hitters and closer to the center fielder for right-handed pull hitters. In addition the right fielder backs up all plays made from the left side of the field.

Short Fielder

The short fielder is the tenth player permitted in slow-pitch softball. This person may play as an extra infielder or outfielder or as a roving player. The exact position is determined by the team preference and/or situation. If the batter is a long-ball hitter, the short fielder may play as an outfielder; if the batter is an excellent place-hitter, then the short fielder may play as an extra infielder. As a rover, the short fielder plays between the infield and outfield, swinging more to the left for right-handed hitters and more to the right for left-handed hitters. The short fielder must be very versatile to be able to fulfill these roles. Speed, agility and a good throwing arm are essential abilities.

No matter what your defensive roles, your ability to throw, to catch, to run, to judge the ball and to think ahead will determine your true effectiveness.

If the hit is to the far center outfield and the situation calls for the fielded ball to be sent to home plate, where should the center fielder throw the ball?

Outfielder Defensive Responsibilities

Outfielders' defensive responsibilities after fielding the ball are to prevent base runners from advancing after catching a fly ball or fielding a base hit, and to back up other outfielders and infielders nearest to them.

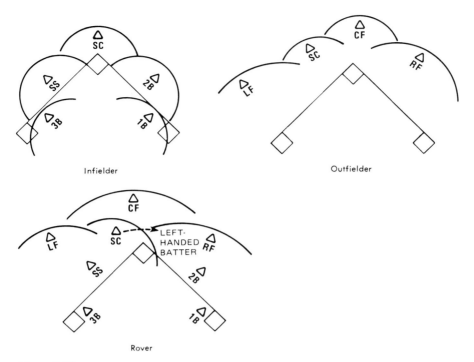

Figure 6.19
Short fielder positions (slow pitch).

Backing

If the ball is not hit directly to you, move quickly to back up any adjacent outfielder or infielder or behind the closest base to which a throw may be made. Inform the fielder what base to throw the ball to if there are base runners.

Holding Runners

After fielding the ball, return the ball one base in advance of the lead base runner to prevent him/her from advancing, or to a player in position to prevent the runner from advancing.

Throwing out Base Runners

Throw the ball hard and low to the base if a putout is possible. If a cutoff play may be necessary, throw on a line just above the head of the cutoff player.

OUTFIELDER PROBLEMS AND CORRECTIONS

Problem	Causes	Corrections
Slow start on the ball	Not paying attention	Concentration and communication from teammates.
Incorrect placement of throw	Poor judgment	Communication from center fielder.

Safety

Outfielders should take the following precautions:

1. Call for the ball to avoid collisions with other fielders.
2. Know at all times where the fences are located. They should be padded for your protection.

When a putout at base is possible, why should the fielding player throw the ball low to the base?

Practice

Individual

Fly Balls

Throw golf balls to yourself at various angles and practice catching them.

Throwing

Take a basket of softballs and practice throwing to the various bases as targets. Practice cutoff throws by placing a 7- to 8-foot marker near the infield and attempting to throw just above it.

Group

Ground Balls

Ground balls are high to the various outfielders who field the ball and throw to the catcher.

Fly Balls

Same as above.

Defensive Position Play 87

Throwing to Bases

All types of hits are made to the outfielders, who are directed to throw the balls to the various bases.

Evaluation

Fielding Record

Keep a record of all errors and play attempts. Divide the errors by total number of attempts. It may be useful to subdivide these totals by type of play such as catching fly balls, fielding base hits and throwing to the base or to a cutoff player.

References

Brace, D. *Skills Test Manual: Softball for Girls and Softball for Boys*. Washington, D.C.: American Association for Health, Physical Education and Recreation, 1966.

Craig, Susan and Johnson, Ken. *The Softball Handbook*. Champaign, Illinois: Leisure Press. 1984.

Drysdale, Sharon J. and Harris, Karen S. *Complete Handbook of Winning Softball*. Boston, Massachusetts: Allyn and Bacon, Inc., 1982.

Feigner, Eddie. *What Little I Know About Pitching and Hitting*. Waller, Washington: Saxum Publishing, 1980.

Killain, Pat. "Speed vs. Accuracy in Teaching the Softball Pitcher." *1979–81 NAGSW Softball Guide*. Washington, D.C.: National Association for Girls' and Women's Sports, American Alliance for Health, Physical Education and Recreation.

Kramer, Betty. "The Cutoff Play and the Relay." *1979–81 NAGSW Softball Guide*. Washington, D.C.: National Association for Girls' and Women's Sports, American Alliance for Health, Physical Education and Recreation.

Lopiano, Donna. "Developing the Exceptional Slingshot Pitcher." *1974–76 Softball Guide*. Washington, D.C.: American Association for Health Physical Education and Recreation.

Ricker, Marge. "The Run-Down Play." *1979–81 NAGSW Softball Guide*. Washington, D.C.: National Association for Girls' and Women's Sports, American Alliance for Health, Physical Education and Recreation.

Schunk, Carol. "Tenth Man Theme." *1972–74 DGWS Softball Guide*. Washington, D.C.: American Association for Health, Physical Education and Recreation.

Webb, Jim. *Learning to Pitch Softball* (Things Every Pitcher, Catcher, and Coach Should Know). Asturia, Illinois: Summertime Books Co., 1982.

Wenk, Robert. *Coaching Youth Softball*. New York, New York: Leisure Press, 1984, Chapters 8, 9, 10, 11, 12, and 13.

Wilson, Jamie. "Tips on Infielding." *1972–74 DGWS Softball Guide*, Washington, D.C.: American Association for Health, Physical Education and Recreation.

Patterns of Play

7

As your skill in the various softball techniques improves, so should your ability to execute these skills in planned offensive and defensive patterns. Your ability to score runs will increase when you are able to take advantage of circumstances that are conducive to getting a base hit or advancing to the next base. You should know how to adjust your position defensively to protect against offensive patterns that could result in the scoring of runs. If you are the pitcher, know the strategy as well as the techniques of pitching.

You will be able to—

1. take advantage of prevailing defensive conditions to enhance opportunities to score runs, and
2. take advantage of prevailing offensive conditions to prevent runs from being scored.

Offensive Patterns

Batting

When batting, your foremost thought should be to get on base. This goal will be achieved most often by getting a base hit. However, an assessment of the prevailing offensive and defensive situations should guide you in deciding on any adjustments in your batting plan. Shortening your grip on the bat so that you can swing the bat faster and more accurately will help you to hit a fastball pitcher or a pitcher with a great deal of "stuff." When the pitcher seems to lack control or seems to be getting tired, try to be very selective in swinging at pitches. It is advisable not to swing at a 3–0 pitch or even a 3–1 pitch, since a walk is likely. However, if you are a power hitter, you could possibly hit a "grooved pitch" (one in the center of the strike zone) for extra bases. As the batter, you have the advantage on a 3–2 pitch since you know that the pitcher must throw the next ball in the strike zone.

As a batter, do you try to adjust to the pitcher and to the situation by changes in your stance, grip, and/or swing? Do you know your batting average? number of runs batted in?

Your second objective should be to advance a base runner. This can be accomplished by sacrificing, by bunting or hitting a fly ball, or by hitting the ball on the ground in the direction away from the base runner that may force the ball to be played only on you, thus allowing the runner to advance. For example, if the runner is on second base and you hit the ball to the right side of the infield, the ball most often would be played at first base to force you, allowing the runner to advance to third base.

For fast pitch only, surprise the defense with a bunt if they are playing back. Conversely, if they are playing in for a bunt, it might be wise to try to punch the ball over their heads. Swing at a pitch, but with no intention of hitting it when you know a base runner is going to steal. The swinging action confuses the catcher and often may result in a poor throw. The usual offensive pattern in a close game is to try to get a runner on base, sacrifice that player to second with a bunt, or have him or her try to steal second base so that a base hit can result in a score.

Another pattern is to score a runner from third base by bunting. This strategy is called by a coach, since both you and the base runner must be in coordination. One attempt is called the *safety squeeze bunt.* You attempt to bunt down the first base line and the runner attempts to score. If you miss the ball, pop it up, or don't bunt, the runner can get back to his or her base. However, on a *suicide squeeze,* you must attempt to bunt the ball wherever it is pitched because the base runner is breaking with the pitch to come home. The strategy is to get the runner home before the ball can be fielded. Often both you and the runner will be safe.

Batting Order

The order in which players are assigned to bat should be carefully determined. The first batter is often the shortest and fastest player on the team, a player who frequently gets on base. The second batter should be a good bunter or hit-and-run hitter. A player should be able to advance the leadoff batter. The third, fourth and fifth batters should be the most consistent and powerful hitters on the team. Their job is to bring home the earlier batters by hitting homers or extra-base hits. The weaker hitters follow. Usually the pitcher bats last.

The offensive team is permitted the option of using a "designated hitter" in fast-pitch play only. A designated hitter becomes the tenth player in the lineup although he or she may bat in any position so indicated at the start of the game and on the lineup sheet. A designated hitter may not enter the game on defense and should be an outstanding hitter.

The offensive team in slow pitch is permitted an "extra hitter." The extra hitter becomes the eleventh player in the lineup although he or she may bat in any position as in fast pitch. An extra hitter may not enter the game on defense and should be an outstanding hitter. The extra hitter differs from a designated hitter in that the extra hitter is not a replacement hitter for a fielder who cannot bat.

Explain the difference between a designated hitter (DH) and an extra hitter (EH).

Figure 7.1
Offensive Patterns: a) Fast-pitch bunt strategy to advanced base runner. b) Sacrifice hitting to advance runner.

Baserunning

At the crack of the bat, have one goal in mind—to get on base. Be alert and take advantage of any misplay to reach the farthest base. When you know you can reach first base safely, immediately round the base and look for the ball and the position of the fielders. If an error occurs, or if you realize that a defensive player cannot cover the base you are attempting to reach, continue running.

Once you are on base, your next goal is to advance around the bases to score a run. Your strategy now is to be aware of the game situation, the ability of the batter, the position of the fielders and the number of outs. Be prepared to advance a base or more on any hit or error. Tag up on any long fly ball so that you may advance a base after the catch. Lead off partway on short fly balls or sinking fly balls in order to advance if the ball is not caught and/or to draw a throw. If you are on third base, stand with one foot on the base and the other in foul territory and move to foul territory as soon as it is legally possible to avoid being hit by a fair ball and being called out. With less than two outs:

1. Runner on first base and the ball is bunted to third base. Be alert to take third base if the catcher or pitcher does not cover the base while the third baseman fields the ball.
2. Runner on first and third base. On a short fly ball to the outfield, tag up and advance to draw the throw to second base so that the runner on third can score.
3. Runners on first and third. The runner on first should advance to second and attempt to draw the long throw, which will permit the runner on third to score.
4. Runner on second base. If the ball is hit deep to the left side of the infield forcing a long throw to first base, try to advance to third base as soon as the ball leaves the fielder's hand.

When there are two outs, run to the next base as soon as the ball is hit. If you are caught in a rundown and are the lead runner with less than two out, attempt to make the next base and do not attempt to return to the original base. The trailing runner should be able to reach that base.

Where should you stand on third base and move to when the ball is pitched or hit?

Coaching

As a base runner you should always watch the coach for signals that indicate you are to steal or run on a "hit-and-run" attempt, or if the batter is to bunt or "take a pitch." In addition, the coach will give you verbal and visual signals to guide decisions to go on, stop, tag up or come back to a base.

Leading Off

Leading off is permitted in fast and 12-inch slow pitch only when the pitcher's non-pivot foot crosses the pitching plate. In 16-inch slow pitch, the batter may lead off at any time and can be "picked off" by the pitcher. The length of the lead off should never exceed the ability to safely return after the ball is pitched in fast and 12-inch slow pitch and before the pitcher addresses the hitter in 16-inch play. In all fast pitch situations, it is important that you look like you are going to steal on every pitch, and equally important when you stop your advance to immediately reverse your weight to the rear foot to avoid "leaning away" and thus losing balance for a fast return to base.

Substitute Players

Substitute or "pinch" hitters are used when a crucial scoring opportunity is at hand and a better hitter, bunter, or a more powerful hitter than the scheduled batter is available and needed. A pinch runner is used if the run is needed and the base runner is slow. The base runner is removed from the game, and a speedier runner is substituted. In fast-pitch and slow-pitch play, any of the starting players except the DH in fast pitch or EH in slow pitch may be withdrawn and reenter once, provided such player occupies the same batting position, whenever he or she is in the lineup. However, a pitcher who is withdrawn cannot return to the pitching position for the remainder of the game. In addition, substitute fielders are used in the late innings by the leading team to remove a "good bat-weak glove person" for a stronger fielder.

In arranging a team's batting order, what are the abilities desired in each of the first five batters?

Defensive Patterns

Many defensive maneuvers are possible to counter offensive strategies. However, regardless of the defensive patterns used, if the offense executes its strategy correctly and accurately, it is very difficult, if not impossible, for the defensive patterns to work.

Fielding

The defensive team employs strategies to offset the offensive patterns of play. The following general rules should be followed:

1. Prevent the base runner from advancing a base. After a fly ball is caught, return the ball immediately to the base ahead of the runner. If a ground ball is hit, fake the runner back to the base before throwing out the batter-base runner. If you cannot throw ahead of the runner, throw the ball to a central position player such as the second baseman or pitcher.
2. Always make the sure out.
3. Always try for more than one out when there are runners on base.

Pitching is often considered the only defense a team has in softball. It is true that effective pitching will prevent base hits, but many base hits are gained simply because the fielders were not in proper position to protect their areas effectively. A good defensive team will alter its positions on the field to counter any offensive situation that might impair defensive efficiency.

There are times when the basic infield positions should be altered so that the infielders play closer or farther from home plate. These positions are called "back," "halfway" and "close in." The *back position* is taken when there is no one on base. The infield and outfield play back, or deep, because the play probably will be to first base. This position enables the fielders to cover more territory. If the batter is left-handed, the infield and outfield shift about five steps toward the right-field line from their normal playing positions. The infielders play several steps behind the base paths.

The *halfway* or *pulled-in position* is assumed when there is a runner on first or second base with less than two outs. This position is also used when a bunt is expected or when the batter is a very fast runner. The halfway position allows for short, quick throws to prevent runners from advancing and also increases the possibility of a double play. In the halfway position, the outfielders move in a few steps, and the first and third basemen move several steps in front of the base path. The second baseman and the shortstop move in a step or two from regular position.

The *close in position* is recommended when there is a runner on third base with less than two outs. This position enables the infield to field the ball rapidly so that they can hold runners on their bases or throw to home plate for an out. In the close position the outfielders move in a few steps, the first and third basemen move approximately one-third the distance from the base path toward home plate, and the shortstop and second baseman move to the base path. If the runner on

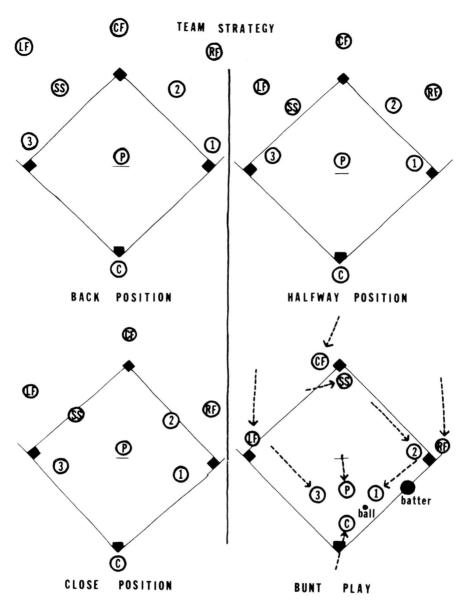

Figure 7.2
Defensive positions.

third is the winning run, the outfielders move closer to the infield. If the fielding team is several runs ahead, however, some teams prefer to play back and attempt to make the surest out even though a run may score.

In addition to shifting positions up and back and sideways, fielders must shift positions to cover bases not assigned to them and to back up plays. Techniques

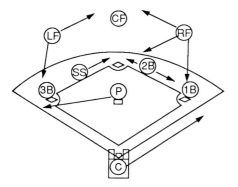

Figure 7.3
Covering and backing.

Figure 7.4
Catcher backing up a play. Play to first base. The catcher backs up the first baseman.

Figure 7.5
Covering first base. The second baseman covers first base when the first baseman must field the bunt.

Figure 7.6
Shortstop covering. When the second baseman must cover first base, the shortstop covers second base.

for backing and covering were discussed in Chapters Five and Six. Since there are many possibilities, figures 7.3–7.13 illustrate where the fielders should move.

Covering and Backing Patterns

Many defensive errors are mental rather than physical errors resulting from not backing up plays and covering bases properly. Practice is constantly needed to make these movements proper and routine. Teammates should shout directions and reminders to each other. Occasionally a timeout will be called to discuss the proper strategy on a possible play.

Under what circumstances should the infielders assume the "back" position? the "halfway" position? the "close in" position?

Patterns of Play 95

Figure 7.7
Pitcher covers home. The pitcher covers home when the catcher is drawn away.

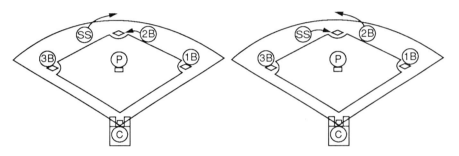

Figure 7.8
Action at second base. Shortstop backs up the second baseman when he/she covers the base, and the second baseman backs up the shortstop when he/she covers second base.

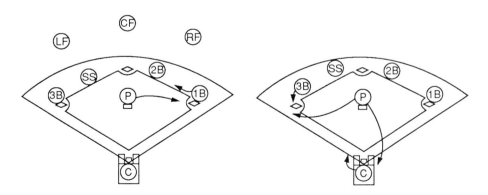

Figure 7.9
Pitcher covering first base. The pitcher covers first base when the first baseman must move to the right to field the ball.

Figure 7.10
Pitcher backing up a play. The pitcher backs up the third baseman on plays to third base and backs up the catcher on throws to home base.

96   *Chapter 7*

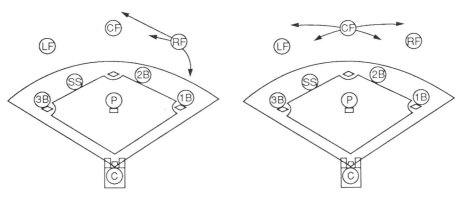

Figure 7.11
Right fielder backing up a play.

Figure 7.12
Center fielder backing up a play.

Figure 7.13
Left fielder backing up a play.

Special Situations

Bunt Coverage

Bunts are usually placed between home and the pitching circle, and along the foul lines. If the ball is rolling or spinning toward the foul line, it is better to let it roll foul. Touch it as soon as it reaches foul territory to make it a dead ball. Attempt to play all other bunts. When a bunt is anticipated, the first and third basemen assume a close-in position and charge the plate as soon as the batter appears to bunt. The pitcher should cover the area directly in front of the pitching circle and the catcher should cover the area immediately in front of the plate. The shortstop and second baseman will have three bases to cover. If there is no runner on second base, the shortstop covers second base and the second baseman first base. If there is a runner on second base, the shortstop covers third base and the second baseman covers first base.

Identify the special abilities needed for the leadoff batter and the third-, fourth- and fifth-place batters.

Priority Plays

Fly balls travel across several positions. To eliminate any confusion, the following priorities are set:

1. Center fielders have priority over other fielders.
2. Outfielders have priority over infielders.
3. Other infielders have priority over pitchers and catchers.
4. The shortstop and second basemen have priority over the first and third basemen on hits behind their base.
5. Catchers have priority for balls hit near home plate.

Always signal visually and verbally that you are taking priority.

Cutoff Plays

Sometimes it can be judged that a throw will not put out the intended runner. Wherever this occurs it should be cutoff and redirected to wherever a more likely out is possible or such an action would prevent a runner from advancing. Throws are most often cutoff going to third base or to home plate. The shortstop and first baseman most often affect the cutoff and the third baseman and catcher usually call the play.

Why should the shortstop and second baseman have priority over the first and third basemen for fly balls hit behind first and third base?

Practice

Individual

Mental Practice

List possible playing situations and attempt to "think through" the play action that you should take from your playing position.

Group

Skill Sessions

The coach or team leader should list various playing situations, both offensive and defensive, and request that players indicate what action they would take. Plays may be diagramed and given to players to study.

Mock Setups

Place the team on the field. The coach, manager, or team leader calls out or sets up various offensive situations for the defensive team to react to.

Bunt Reaction Drill

Place infielders in their assigned positions. The coach pre-announces the number of outs and the bases occupied. The pitcher pitches to the coach who bunts. The players charge the bunt, field the ball, and other infielders cover and back up the proper bases. The ball is bunted in all directions. After three tries in each direction, the players switch positions.

Backing up Practice

All players take their positions. No ball is used. The coach identifies a situation and points where the ball is hit. All players react and move to their proper positions. Later, the coach hits the ball, runners start from home and advance as in game conditions. Fielders will move to their proper fielding, covering and backing positions.

Rundown Practice

Set up a situation between pairs of bases. Have the infielders make the play with proper positioning and backing up. The goal should be to complete the play with only two throws.

References

Craig, Susan and Johnson, Ken. *The Softball Book*. West Point, New York: Leisure Press, 1984, Chapters 15 and 16.

Fortune, Annette. *Complete Softball*. Windsor, Connecticut: Jet Press, 1982.

Jones, Billie J. and Murray, Mary Jo. *Softball: Concepts for Coaches and Teachers*. Dubuque, Iowa: William C. Brown Company Publishers, 1982.

Houseworth, Steven D. and Rivkin, Francine V. *Coaching Softball Effectively*. Champaign, Illinois: Human Kinetics Publishers, Inc., 1985. Chapters 2 and 7.

Teaching, Coaching, and Managing

Your progress may be speeded up or helped if you are given expert assistance from a teacher-coach or manager, or you may speed up the progress of young players by utilizing effective instructional and management procedures.
You will be able to—

1. plan and provide meaningful learning experiences,
2. improve the individual and team play of performers,
3. organize and conduct team play to maximize opportunities to win.

Respect for and acceptance of the teacher-coach are essential and are fostered through demonstrated knowledge of the game and firm but fair treatment of the players. A successful teacher-coach accurately diagnoses the needs of the player and prescribes meaningful learning experiences. In addition, good judgment, a sense of humor and a positive self-concept are important personal traits that can inspire the desire to learn and the will to succeed.

Planning

Instructional plans are usually based upon the age, ability and interest of the learner. Listed below is a suggested progression of skills for various age groups.

Elementary School	Junior High School	High School and College
Throwing	Batting: grips, bunting	Batting: hit-and-run, fake bunting, drag bunting, place-hitting
Catching	Baserunning: leadoff, stealing bases	
Fielding		Baserunning: rounding, sliding
Running	Throwing:overhand, sidearm, underhand	Throwing: sidearm, cutoff
Batting		
Basic rules	Fielding: grounders, fly balls, backing, use of mitt and glove, tagging	Fielding: charging, reading conditions
Leadup games		
	Position play: covering area, duties	Strategy
	Official rules	Patterns of play
	Slow-pitch game	Official rules: advanced rules
	Soft-softball fast-pitch game	Umpiring

101

Managing Duties

The teacher-coach or the manager is responsible for the overall operation of the team, which includes the selection of the team, conditioning, instruction and conduct of the game. As a coach or manager, you must have not only a thorough knowledge of your team but also of the opposition. This knowledge will assist you in deciding lineups, pitching changes, pinch hitters, runners and fielding maneuvers. Decisions need to be made and communicated to the team concerning (1) their defensive positions, (2) where a play is to be made, (3) the likelihood of a bunt or steal, 4) plans to steal and so forth. These decisions will be based upon a careful analysis of the following points:

Pitcher:	control, style, "stuff," and fielding ability
Catcher:	throwing ability, agility, alertness, and backing of first base
Infielders:	position, throwing ability, covering, and backing excellence
Out-fielders:	field condition, speed, and throwing ability.

Promote improved play by reviewing the game with the team immediately after completion. Compliment good play but avoid placing blame and criticizing mistakes. Explain proper actions and prescribe special help and practice for consistent performance failures.

Team Selection

You should select team members on the following bases: (1) apparent natural ability as demonstrated by ease and correctness when throwing, fielding and hitting, (2) speed and hitting, (3) strong and accurate throwing, (4) dependability and dedication and (5) team needs. Although all of the above criteria are important, dependability and dedication can transform a below-average player into one possessing acceptable abilities.

Conditioning

Getting the team ready for play requires preseason conditioning and pregame warm-up. *Preseason conditioning* should include several weeks of flexibility, strength and endurance training. As a general rule, players should at least three times a week do static stretches in all muscle groups; progressively overload the capacity of the major muscle groups by increasing sets of exercises, the repetitions and the load; and running a mile. The *pregame warm-up* should include loosening up arms and legs by stretching, throwing and running. Infielders need practice in fielding grounders from their position and throwing to various bases. The outfielders should practice catching fly balls and line drives and returning throws. The pitcher needs several minutes of progressively more demanding and accurate practice.

Figure 8.1
Team meeting.

Instruction

Instruction should be the major goal of practice. The amount of practice depends upon the level of play and age of the players. Usually teams will practice from 3 to 5 days a week for two to three hours. It is important to adhere to the following principles to guide instruction and practice:

1. Plan each practice to make the most of the time.
2. Secure one coach or teacher for every four or five players.
3. Plan to keep all players active and busily engaged in improving their play.
4. Vary the practice to include new skills and yet sufficient repetition to reinforce skills.
5. Emphasize defensive practice early in the season and offensive practice later. Organize offensive practice to minimize inactivity.

Practice

Individual and group practice drills and tasks have been suggested in earlier chapters. Maximize practice as much as possible. You should work with the learner to identify specific goals to be achieved.

Class Organization

Listed below is a suggested lesson plan for a 45-minute class:

Stretching and warm-up exercises	5–10 minutes
Review and practice skills	5–10 minutes
Plan individual and group tasks with identified goals.	
Introduce new skills (bunting)	5 minutes
Demonstrate, explain and/or have available other input sources.	
Practice bunting	5–10 minutes
Work in groups of three. Hit five and rotate.	
Game play	15–20 minutes
Play bunt game.	

Team Organization

Preseason practice should begin four to six weeks before the schedule begins. Early meetings should stress conditioning, light throwing, and running. A typical practice session may be as follows:

Warm-ups and conditioning	15 minutes
Batting practice	60 minutes
Pitchers rotate every 20 minutes.	
Fielders play position and make directed plays.	
Batters are directed to hit a certain number of hits.	
Specific skill practice is conducted.	
Infield and outfield practice	45 minutes

The ball is batted over the left fielder's head. What directions should the first base coach be giving to the batter-base runner? Why?

Conduct of the Game

As soon as possible inform the players of the starting lineup. Always look ahead to your team and the opponent's next hitters in order to plan any needed substitutions. Direct the coaches as to offensive strategy and the fielders as to defensive strategy. React positively to events good or bad and communicate with players concerning their feelings and ideas. Project a winning attitude and be sure you know the rules. After the game discuss with the team their successes and failures.

Coaching Duties

The rules permit one member of the offensive team to stand at the sidelines by first base and another by third base. These coaches may be players, coaches, managers, or other personnel connected with the team. They must not interfere with play, but they may direct the batting and running activities of the team.

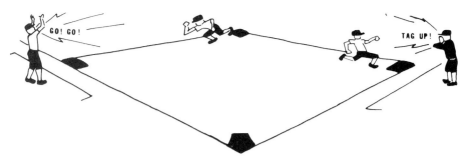

Figure 8.2
Using coaches.

The coaches shout words of encouragement to the batter and give the batter directions by the use of certain words or signs. Coaches assist the base runners in the proper running of the bases by shouting directions to them. A good coach must be able to make quick decisions. The coach assumes a position in the coach's box that will permit him or her to see the runners and fielders easily. Coaches give signs to the batter and direct his or her running on the base. The third base coach usually gives the signs to the batter. Keep the same sign for a particular action but vary preceding and succeeding signs. This will confuse the opposition but not your team. Signals include touching the ear, chin, nose, belt buckle or placing hands together, on the knees, head and so forth.

Safety

The following basic rules will help to ensure the safety of everyone playing softball:

1. Do not allow jewelry to be worn during play or practice.
2. Plan adequate warm-up time.
3. Arrange practice drills so that batted or thrown balls will not hit performers.
4. Arrange practice so that each team is seated at least 20 feet behind home plate and behind the foul line.

References

Craig, Susan and Johnson, Ken. *The Softball Handbook*. West Point, New York: Leisure Press, 1984, Chapter 1.

Johnson, Carol Peterson with Wright, Margie. *The Woman's Softball Book*. New York, New York: Leisure Press, 1984, Chapter 1.

Potter, Diane and Brockmeyer, Gretchen. *Softball-Steps to Success*. Champaign, Illinois: Leisure Press, 1989.

Wenk, Robert. *Coaching Youth Softball*. West Point, New York: Leisure Press, 1984, Chapter 15.

Rules and Unwritten Laws of the Game

9

Softball is governed essentially by one official set of rules, which include the following games: 11 and 12-inch slow pitch, last pitch, 16-inch slow pitch, modified pitch and co-ed play. In addition, after one hundred years, softball is also unofficially controlled by many unwritten rules.

You will be able to—

1. play softball according to the official rules, and
2. understand and follow unwritten softball rules.

Rules of the Game

Prior to 1980, all softball rules were under the jurisdiction of the International Joint Rule Committee on Softball. Since that time they have been under the jurisdiction of the Amateur Softball Association. A committee for each type of game sets the rules. Each committee has representation from the various game committees, the ASA umpires and allied organizations. These committees meet annually to review softball playing rules and to make any needed changes. The rules identified in this chapter represent what was current at the time of writing. Permission to copy the rules must be given by the ASA. A complete set of rules can be secured from local sporting goods dealers, bookstores, or from your local library.

The Playing Field

Softball should be played in a clear and unobstructed area within a radius which varies by gender, age and type of play. The distance ranges from 300 feet for slow-pitch super play, to 175 feet for girls 12 years old and under, from home plate between foul lines. Pitching distance for fast-pitch women and junior play is 40 feet, and for boys and girls ages 10 and under the distance is 35 feet. The pitching distance is 46 feet for adult and junior men in slow-pitch play. Sixteen-inch slow-pitch play uses 38 feet. The official ASA rules should be checked since there are many variations depending upon gender, age and type of play. For example, the National Association for Intercollegiate Athletics (NAIA) and the National Collegiate Athletic Association (NCAA) use 43 feet for their official pitching distance.

A batter's box that is 3 feet wide and 7 feet long is marked off on either side of home plate. A catcher's box and coaches' box must be marked off also. When deviations from these dimensions must be made, special ground rules may be agreed upon.

Figure 9.1
Official dimensions for softball diamonds.

Figure 9.2
Dimensions.

Rules and Unwritten Laws of the Game 109

Players and Substitutes

A team shall consist of nine (fast pitch) or ten (slow pitch) players whose positions shall be designated as follows: pitcher, catcher, first baseman, second baseman, third baseman, shortstop, left fielder, center fielder and right fielder. If a designated hitter is used in the fast-pitch games, he/she becomes the tenth player. In the slow-pitch game, the tenth player shall be designated as a short fielder. Each player traditionally covers a certain specified area but may be stationed anywhere on fair ground except for the pitcher, who must be in legal pitching position, and the catcher, who must be in his/her box.

Substitute players may be used, but once removed from the game a player may not return. Substitute players may be put in the game for a batter, fielder, runner, or pitcher. The position of a player may be altered at any time during a game, but a substitute player must assume the position in the batting order of the player he/she replaced. However, in fast-pitch play only, any of the *starting* players except the pitcher and DH (designated hitter) may be withdrawn and re-enter once, provided such player occupies the same batting position when he/she is in the lineup.

Slow-pitch play allows an eleventh player who may not play defensively. This player is called an EH (extra hitter).

The Game

The home team bats last in each inning; however, if neither team is designated as a "home" team, the choice is determined by the toss of a coin. A game is complete when seven innings have been played. If the home team is leading, however, the last half of the seventh inning is not played. If the game should be tied at the end of seven innings, play continues until one side has scored more runs than the other at the end of a complete inning.

Occasionally a game cannot be completed because of weather, darkness, or calamities. In such cases, the decision to terminate the game is made by the umpire. If five or more innings have been played, the game is considered a regulation, completed game. A game may be forfeited by the umpire in favor of the team not at fault for failure to appear to play, for delaying or unduly hastening the game, for willful violation of a rule after warning, or for fewer than nine (fast pitch) or ten (slow pitch) players on a team.

The winner of the game is the team that scores the most runs in a regulation game. One run is scored each time a base runner legally touches each base consecutively before the third out of the inning.

Pitching Regulations

The game starts when the umpire calls "Play!" The first batter steps into the batter's box, the catcher readies himself or herself in the catcher's box, and the pitcher in fast pitch takes a position with pivot foot on the pitcher's plate and non-pivot foot on or behind the pitcher's plate. Both feet must be on the ground within the 24-inch length of the pitcher's plate. In slow-pitch play both feet must

110   *Chapter 9*

be on the ground with one or both feet in contact with the rubber. The ball may be held no less than one second or more than ten seconds. The pitcher may use any windup provided he or she does not make any motion to pitch without immediately delivering the ball to the batter, use a rocker action, make more than one revolution of the arm, make any motion that results in a reversal of the forward action or continue to windup after taking the forward step. In the slow-pitch game, the ball must be delivered at a moderate speed with a perceptible arc (from the time it leaves the pitcher's hand) of at least 6 feet before the ball reaches home plate.

When the pitch is delivered, the batter must decide whether or not to swing the bat at the ball in an attempt to hit it. If the pitch is not struck at, the umpire decides whether the pitch is a ball or a strike. If the batter incurs three strikes, he/she is called out; conversely, if the batter acquires four balls, he/she is entitled to first base and becomes a base runner. If the pitcher delivers the ball illegally by dropping, rolling, or bouncing the ball to prevent the batter from striking it, or if tape or other substances are used on the ball, a ball is called on the batter. In the fast-pitch game only, base runners are permitted to advance one base.

Batting Regulations

If the batter elects to swing at the pitch and misses it, a strike is called. A foul ball is declared if the ball is hit but lands outside the lines defining the playing field. When a foul ball is not caught on the fly, a strike is called unless the batter already has two strikes. In this case any number of foul balls may be hit without a strike being called in fast pitch. In slow-pitch play, a foul ball not caught is always a strike including the third strike. A foul tip is called if the ball is hit and goes directly back to the catcher's hands and is held by the catcher. A foul tip is a strike regardless of the number of strikes on the batter. When a fly ball is caught, whether it is in fair or foul territory, the batter is out. If the batter hits the ball on the ground into fair territory, he or she must reach first base before the ball can be held by the first baseman while touching the bag, or be declared out. Each team is given three outs during its time at bat. The batter is out when any of the following situations occur: when three strikes are called and the ball is held by the catcher; when a foul ball is legally caught; immediately when he or she hits an infield fly with base runners on first and second or first, second and third bases with less than two outs; or when the ball is bunted in foul territory when the batter has two strikes (fast pitch only). The batter is out in slow-pitch softball if he or she chops downward on the ball or attempts to bunt the pitch.

Baserunning Regulations

The batter becomes a base runner as soon as a ball is hit into fair territory, or when four balls have been called, or when the catcher interferes with or prevents the batter from striking a pitched ball. In addition, in fast pitch the batter becomes a base runner when hit by a pitched ball or when the catcher drops the third strike when no one is on base or in any situation when there are two outs. Bases must be touched consecutively. Two base runners may not occupy the same

Rules and Unwritten Laws of the Game   111

base. The right to a base is given to the runner who first occupied it, and he or she is entitled to hold that base until he or she has legally touched the next base or until forced to vacate it for a succeeding runner.

The base runner is entitled to advance with liability to be put out when the heel of his or her non-pivot foot crosses the front edge of the pitcher's plate on the forward step on a pitch (fast pitch only), when the ball is overthrown into fair or foul territory and is not blocked, when the ball is batted into fair territory and is not blocked, and when a legally caught fly ball is first touched. In the fast-pitch game leading off is legal after the ball leaves the pitcher's hand. However, the base runner must return to the base if he or she does not steal once the pitcher has the ball within the 8-foot radius of the pitcher's plate.

Base runners are entitled to advance to another base and may not be put out in the following situations: when forced to vacate a base because the batter was awarded a base on balls, when a field obstructs the base runner's path, when the catcher interferes with the batter, and when a pitcher or overthrown ball in foul territory is blocked or obstructed. In addition, base runners may advance without being put out if the batter is awarded a base because he or she was hit by a pitched ball, when a wild pitch or passed ball goes under, over, or through the backstop, and when the pitcher pitches illegally.

When does the batter become a base runner after the third strike in fast-pitch softball?

There are times when a base runner is restricted to a certain number of bases. For example, if the fence is less than the prescribed distance from home base, a ball falling beyond it will entitle the runner to only two bases. If the fence is regulation distance, but the ball rolls or bounds into a stand or over, under, or through a fence or other obstruction marking the boundaries, two bases are awarded. When the team at bat commits an illegal act, a base runner cannot advance on the play. Thus, if a ball is illegally batted or if the batter interferes with a play, no advance is permitted. In order to protect the defensive team, if the umpire is struck by a batted ball before it is touched by a fielder or if the plate umpire interferes with the catcher's attempt to throw, no advance is permitted.

A base runner is declared out if he or she is not standing on a base and is touched by a fielder who is holding the ball or if forced to advance and fails to reach that base before the ball is held on that base by a fielder. A base runner also will be called out if he or she runs the base in reverse order, fails to return to his or her base when play is resumed after a suspension of play, passes a preceding base runner, leaves a base before a fly ball has been caught, fails to touch a base, is struck by a batted ball, or interferes with the fielding of a batted ball.

Official Rules

The ASA Official Rules are most often used to govern play. These rules specify variations for the following levels of play: adult fast and slow pitch for men and women, slow pitch for co-ed and super play, modified and 16-inch slow pitch for men and women and for youth play for slow and fast pitch for boys and girls ages 12 and under, 15 and under and 18 and under. Because of these variations it is important that you obtain the latest official rule book to be able to play *your* game according to the correct rules.

However, two variations are so different that they are worth pointing out.

Co-ed Play

The ASA Rules Committee has developed rules governing co-ed slow-pitch softball play. Essentially these rules call for foul lines 275 feet from home plate to the fence, 46 feet pitching distance, no metal or hard plastic spikes and ten players. The ten players must include five males and five females playing at all times. In addition, there must be two of each gender in the outfield and in the infield. The battery shall consist of one male and one female. The batting order must alternate each batter by gender.

What organization's softball rules are most often used in competitive play?

Sixteen-Inch Slow Pitch

The 16-inch slow-pitch game permits base runners to lead off base and pitchers to use two hesitations before delivering the ball to the batter. During these hesitations, the pitcher may attempt to pick off a runner as in baseball. In addition, the bases are 55 feet apart, and the pitching distance is only 35 feet from home plate. Neither gloves nor mitts are permitted.

Officiating

The rules of the game are enforced by one or more umpires. They have the power to order a player or coach to act in any manner that, in their judgment, is necessary to give force and effect to one or all of the rules. An umpire must not be connected in any way with either team. If there are two umpires each has the power to make decisions on violations committed anytime during time or during suspension of play. One umpire rules from behind the plate and the other from the bases. The plate umpire has full charge and is responsible for the conduct of the game. The plate umpire makes decisions on the pitches and the action of the batter. The base umpire renders decisions at all bases except at home plate. In tournament play, usually an umpire is assigned to each base.

Both the ASA and the NAGWS sponsor programs to prepare, assist and regulate umpiring in softball. Questions concerning rules should be sent to The Amateur Softball Association, 2801 NE 50th Street, Oklahoma City, Oklahoma, 73111.

Scorekeeping

The rules specifically outline procedures and regulations for scorekeeping. The official scorer records and summarizes the game activities as they relate to final score, runs batted in, hits, extra-base hits, stolen bases, sacrifice bunts and flies, double plays, triple plays, runners left on base, bases on balls, strikeouts, wild pitches, passed balls, name of the winning pitcher, name of losing pitcher, names of umpires and length of the game.

Sample Game

White City is playing Greenville at Greenville. Since Greenville is playing in its hometown, it is considered the home team and will bat last in each inning. The umpires arrive thirty minutes before the game in order to become familiar with the playing field and the teams.

Just before play begins, the umpires meet with the managers and team captains to go over ground rules. At the time designated to begin the game, the home team assumes its playing field positions. The visiting team bats first and in the order listed on the official batting lineup. The first batter hits the ball on the ground to the third baseman. He or she throws the ball to the first baseman who, while holding the ball, touches the bag ahead of the batter-base runner. This of course is an out. The next batter hits the ball over the shortstop's head; the ball lands before the left fielder can catch it. The left fielder knows the ball cannot get to first base before the batter-base runner, so he throws the ball to the second baseman to prevent the runner from taking an additional base. The next batter receives four balls and is given first base. The runner on first is allowed to take second base. On the next pitch, the batter hits a fly ball, which is caught by the second baseman. There are now two outs. After taking two strikes, the sixth batter hits a ball that the center fielder drops for an error. The base runner on second scores on the error, and the batter-base runner gets to second base while the runner on first base stops at third. The last batter hits a foul ball that is caught by the catcher. This completes the first half of the first inning. The game continues in this manner until completed.

Unwritten Laws

Many softball procedures are accepted by players and fans alike, even though they are not listed in the official rules. Protesting close decisions made by the umpire, shouting words of encouragement and taunting the opposition are acceptable. Players often follow certain superstitions and employ procedures and tactics that might delay or speed up the game.

Conduct of the Game

Protesting decisions is usually considered poor sportsmanship in most athletic endeavors, but in softball such protests are accepted as part of the color of the game in nonschool game situations. Usually these protests do not result in a changed decision. Complaints are actually expected by fans, players and officials. In educational settings, coaches and teachers should discourage adherence to the above unwritten law. Protesting too vigorously or using physical violence will result, however, in the offender's being ejected from the game by the umpire. This behavior is not considered sportsmanlike.

Shouting words of encouragement by teammates to the pitcher or the batter is expected and desirable. Occasionally disparaging remarks are made about the opposing pitcher or batter. These are not considered proper.

Stopping play to discuss the course of action to be taken is legal and is expected in certain situations. The manager may stop play to discuss offensive strategy with his/her batter, or may choose to stop play to discuss defensive strategy when his/her team is in the field. Opposing fans usually boo mildly at these delays but cheer such delays when they are employed by their coaches. The rules limit conferences with the manager or other representatives from the dugout to one per inning.

Conferences occasionally are designed merely to delay the game for a psychological effect. A meeting of the pitcher and catcher is often held to give the pitcher a chance to calm down and rest or to "cool off" the opposition if they have been hitting the pitcher too frequently. The batter tries to annoy the pitcher by meeting with his/her coach or by stepping out of the batting box frequently.

Many players follow certain superstitions that they are certain affect the outcome of the game. For example, some players when running out to their defensive positions feel that they will have bad luck if they don't step on a certain base or hitch their belts before every new batter comes to bat.

Can you describe two unwritten softball laws that are unacceptable in educational situations?

Miscellaneous Laws

Rubbing dirt on the bat is done to dry perspiration so that the bat will not slip from the hands. The pitcher often uses rosin on his/her hands for the same reason.

The next batter to bat is said to be "on deck." When "on deck," the player kneels halfway between the bench and plate, warmed-up and ready to take his/her turn.

If the pitcher gets on base, play usually is stopped to give the pitcher his/her jacket. This is done to keep his/her pitching arm warm so it will not tighten up.

Throwing a bat is dangerous. Players should drop the bat and run to first base when the ball is hit. The bat should not be thrown unnecessarily or in anger.

Most teams wear uniforms to identify themselves with their team. These uniforms are usually the traditional baseball uniform or slacks.

References

National Association for Girls' and Women's Sports. *Softball Guide.* Washington, D.C.: American Alliance for Health, Physical Education and Recreation (published biannually).

Rittler, Kathy. *Official's Manual: Softball.* West Point, New York: Leisure Press, 1982.

Softball Rules Guide. Oklahoma City, Oklahoma: Amateur Softball Association (published yearly).

Playing the Game

10

Softball provides action and excitement that may lead to awards and national and international recognition. Competition is provided on a local, regional, state, national and international basis.
You will be able to—

1. get into condition and improve your game performance,
2. find opportunities to play softball,
3. secure information about current softball developments.

Self-Evaluation

If you wish to develop skill as a softball player, you should know what skill looks like. Try to watch experts play. Read books or articles written about the position you play as well as about the game in general. Set batting, baserunning and fielding goals for yourself. Know your batting average. You can figure it by dividing the total number of hits you have made by the total number of times you have been at bat. A batting average of .300 or more is considered excellent. Fielding average is computed by dividing your total putouts and assists by your total putouts, assists and errors. A fielding average of .970 or better is considered excellent. Clock your running time from home to first and from home to the other bases. Constantly strive to improve that time.

No matter how much you know about softball or how much you practice, your progress toward increased ability in performing softball skills depends on how much effort and time you are willing to give.

How rapidly you master the skills of softball depends on many factors. Needless to say, every athlete would like to find a shortcut to the acquisition of skill. Most, however, would agree that there is no quick, simple way to stardom, but there are some steps that can speed up progress. The first step is to be in top physical condition so that you have the agility, endurance and strength necessary to perform softball techniques. Conditioning is the foundation for perfecting skills. The real work is practice. Individual and group practice, faithfully pursued, will increase skill. In addition, a softball player must study the game and study himself/herself. Only by knowing all the finer points of the game and understanding your own strengths and weaknesses can you intelligently progress toward real skill in playing softball.

Conditioning

Conditioning has three major aspects: physical, nutritional and psychological. These are interdependent, each depending on the other for optimal performance.

Physical

To be an expert softball player you must possess arm and shoulder strength for throwing and batting. Endurance and speed are important to fielding and baserunning. Timing, agility and accuracy are necessary for batting and throwing. Exercise and practice should be pursued beyond the initial point of fatigue if improvement is to be expected. Exercises used for most sports have application to conditioning for softball. As in any sport, however, the exercises should relate to the specific sport. To improve shoulder strength, do up to fifty push-ups; modified push-ups are recommended for those with weaker arms and shoulders.

Endurance, leg strength and speed can be developed by running or jumping rope. A softball player should work toward running at least four times around the field each day or jumping rope for fifteen to twenty minutes. Baserunning is excellent for conditioning the legs for softball play. Stretching and bending exercises will improve flexibility and agility. Hand strength can be improved by squeezing a small rubber ball. Develop your own series of conditioning exercises and do them daily. Do not be content with merely doing the same amount each day. Set goals for yourself to improve your strength, speed and the distance and accuracy of your throws.

In addition to these general conditioning exercises it is recommended that you practice with a weighted bat, weighted ball and wrist snap bat.

Weighted Bats

These can be made by drilling a hole in the barrel and adding lead, or by attaching a weight batting ring. Practice swinging with a weighted bat; this helps to increase the strength of the muscles involved in the swing. The ASA rules limit warming up before officially batting to the use of two official softball bats at once or one ASA approved *warm-up bat*. Official warm-up bats are so marked, weigh a minimum of 48 ounces and have a 2 ½-inch diameter barrel, a no more than 15-inch safety grip and are of one piece construction. These bats are also good for pre-game swing practice.

Weighted Balls

Throwing a heavier ball several times daily will increase your arm strength. A ball can be made heavier by soaking it in water or wrapping tape around it. Increase the distance from the target when speed and accuracy are attained from a particular distance.

Wrist Snap Bats

Wrist snap is important for developing power when batting. A wrist snap bat has a ball attached by a nylon cord placed through a hole in the center of the ball and 1 ½ inches from the end of the bat, about 6 inches from the barrel end. As you swing the bat, the ball will flip in front of the bat as you snap your wrists. This action provides you with feedback regarding the effectiveness of your wrist action.

Imagine yourself in your usual position on the fielding team. There is one out and a runner on first. Can you self-talk to effectively prepare for what may happen with the next batter?

Nutritional

Exercising without control of the diet will ultimately be counterproductive. Proper nutrition means controlling the quantity and quality of what you eat. The quantity of what you eat can be controlled by at least weighing yourself weekly. Like computing your batting average it will tell you whether your food intake is too much or too little. The adjustment in quantity should be equally distributed in the kinds of foods that you eat . . . the quality. Quality nutrition means eating some fruit, vegetables, meat or fish, breads or cereals and milk.

Psychological

Concentration and anxiety control are essential to optimal performance. Concentration can be aided by using *self-talk* and *imagery*. Self-talk is talking to yourself about where you should play, what to expect, what you plan to do and how you wish to feel. Imagery is rehearsing in your mind the exact sequences of a skill, the feeling of a perfectly executed swing or catch and/or the visual "seeing" yourself performing perfectly. Anxiety may aid or harm performance. Accuracy-type skills need less stress; power skills, like running bases, need more stress. Too much stress can be controlled by using the relaxation techniques of deep breathing or alternately tensing and releasing the muscles of the body. The psyching up that can result from cheering, clapping, and bounding up and down adds more stress and power.

Design a personal conditioning program to prepare yourself for a season of softball playing.

Competitive Play

Softball competition begins with the friendly game at the park and ends with World Softball Tournaments for all levels of play. Between these extremes are intramural softball, interscholastic and intercollegiate play, church leagues, park leagues, and industrial play. Many non-school teams are commercially sponsored.

Although the ASA is the governing body for most non-school related competition, other agencies frequently develop their own rules and competitive regulations. The respective State High School Associations under the auspices of the National Federation of High School Activities Association direct most interscholastic play, and the National Collegiate Athletics Association directs intercollegiate state, regional and national championships.

Any organization may form a league and sponsor competition whether it be a school, church, park, or industry. The league does not have to affiliate with the Amateur Softball Association unless it wishes to compete in the Amateur Softball Association tournaments. A group that wishes to compete with other highly skilled players should affiliate with the Amateur Softball Association and play on a statewide or nationwide level.

Membership in the Amateur Softball Association will provide a listing of affiliated teams and their locations, opportunity to participate in clinics, and assistance in local league organization and operation. A copy of the monthly newspaper, *Balls and Strikes,* is sent to members. The newspaper covers local, national and world softball news. The ASA also publishes the official rules in a guide that contains playing rules, articles of general interest, photos, and statistics of slow- and fast-pitch world tournaments.

The United States Slow Pitch Softball Association (USSPSA) also promotes rules, league and tournament play.

In addition, a monthly softball magazine is available, which is called *Softball Insight.*[1] This magazine is in full color, approximately 100 pages in length, and covers all aspects of softball.

The International Softball Federation (ISF) encourages the growth of softball as a worldwide sport. It has secured an agreement with the Olympic Committee to allow softball to be a demonstration sport at the 1992 Olympics.

The International Softball Congress (ISC) was founded in 1946. It is a fast-pitch-only organization with members from the United States, Canada and Mexico. The ISC sponsors area tournaments with winners advancing toward a world tournament. It publishes an annual yearbook.

Softball Organizations Addresses:

Amateur Softball Association
and the International Softball
   Federation
2801 N.E. 50th Street
Oklahoma City, Oklahoma, 73111

International Softball Congress
6007 E. Hillcrest Circle
Anaheim Hills, California, 92807

All participants from the lowly sandlots to the championship playing field agree that softball brings enduring friendships, provides exercise, emphasizes good sportsmanship and is good fun.

1. *Softball Insight,* 1500 Second Ave., S.E. Suite 102B, Cedar Rapids, Iowa 52403

References

National Association for Girls' and Women's Sports. *Softball Guide.* Washington, D.C.: American Alliance for Health, Physical Education, Recreation and Dance (published biannually).

Rittler, Kathy. *Official's Manual: Softball.* West Point, New York: Leisure Press, 1982.

Softball, A Game for Everyone. Oklahoma City, Oklahoma: Amateur Softball Association, 1977.

Softball Rules Guide. Oklahoma City, Oklahoma: Amateur Softball Association (published yearly).

Umpiring and Scorekeeping

11

Quality softball play requires quality umpiring and scorekeeping. After learning about softball, you may wish to become an umpire or scorekeeper.
You will be able to—

1. umpire softball games and
2. keep score for softball games.

Umpiring

Umpiring is a difficult task but it can be enjoyable and rewarding. A thorough understanding of the rules governing play and umpiring, ability to maintain alertness, exercising patience, and making consistent and accurate judgments are essential. Sponsoring agencies such as leagues, associations, or tournaments usually set the minimum standards that govern the quality of umpiring. Obviously less rigor is demanded in "sandlot" play or in physical education classes than in inter-school, league, or tournament competition. Umpires are assigned to a particular game by the organizations they represent.

Number and Position of Umpires

The major function of umpiring is to enforce the rules as they relate to batting, pitching, fielding and baserunning. The number of umpires used in a game depends upon the quality of play. Most games use two umpires. However, a minimum of three umpires are recommended in tournament play.

Major duties are to judge the pitches, hits and render base decisions. When more than one umpire is used, one is called the plate umpire and the other, the base umpire. They both are empowered to order the commission and omission of any act that in their judgment is necessary to comply with the rules.

General Information

The rules clearly identify the duties and responsibilities of umpires. Umpires are expected to wear uniforms consisting of powder-blue shirts and dark navy-blue pants. The plate umpire must wear a mask with a throat protector and body protector in fast-pitch softball and their use is recommended in slow-pitch play. In addition, the plate umpire needs a ball and strike indicator, a whisk broom and a ball bag. Each umpire should have a copy of the official rules available.

Umpires should confer with each other, coaches, managers and scorekeepers before the game begins. The plate umpire collects the games balls and returns them to the owner, and often checks the scorebook with the scorekeeper. All questions should be answered politely during and after the game. The following suggestions will contribute to quality umpiring:

1. Display dignified manner.
2. Call plays consistently, fairly, promptly and accurately.
3. Try to anticipate play in order to be ready for action.
4. Correct errors promptly.
5. Avoid arguments and making personal comments.
6. Be aloof and apart from players, coaches, managers and spectators.
7. Use signals and call out decisions loudly.
8. Attend clinics to update and improve your ability to umpire.

Each umpire has the power to make decisions on violations committed at any time until the game is over. Neither umpire can set aside or question decisions made by the other within the limits of their respective duties. Umpires may consult each other, but the final decision rests with the umpire whose exclusive authority it was to make the decision. All umpires have equal authority to call a runner out for leaving a base too soon, call TIME, remove players, coaches or managers, and call illegal pitches.

Pregame Duties

Umpires should arrive 20–30 minutes before the game is to begin. Prior to the game you as an umpire should ready your equipment, check the playing area to determine needed ground rules, check with the official scorekeeper and the other umpire. A pregame conference is conducted at home plate with the team captains and managers to receive the lineup cards, go over the ground rules, clarify any needed rule interpretation, and indicate expected player behavior.

What are ground rules? When are they reviewed?

Plate Umpire

The plate umpire is considered to be the umpire in chief and is in full charge of the proper conduct of the game. He or she is positioned one or two feet behind the catcher in a crouched position that will not interfere with the catcher's ability to view the plate, batter, pitcher, foul lines, bases and field. Duties of the plate umpire are as follows:

1. Call balls and strikes.
2. Call hit balls, fair or foul.
3. Call legal or illegal pitches and catches.
4. Call base play if the base umpire leaves the infield.
5. Judge whether a ball is bunted, chopped, or touches the batter or clothing of the batter.

Figure 11.1
Plate umpire position.

6. Judge a fly ball as in the infield or outfield.
7. Determine when a game is forfeited.
8. Assume all duties when assigned as a single umpire.
9. Rule on fitness of field for play in case of rain or other problems.
10. Rectify any situation in which the reversal of an umpire's decision or a delayed call by an umpire places a batter-runner or a base runner in jeopardy.

Position

The plate umpire moves into a slight crouch when the pitcher steps on the rubber and assumes a readiness-to-pitch position. Eyes should be fixed on the pitcher and the ball. The body should be aligned with the pitch. Crouch lower, straighter or higher to align the body with the pitch. On a batted ball, the plate umpire takes a position in foul territory, no more than 5 feet down the baseline, in the direction of the next possible play. Umpires may rotate as provided in the rules.

Controlling the Game

The following procedures will contribute to a smooth and safe conduct of the game:

1. Encourage players to hustle on and off the field.
2. Discourage lengthy conferences between players and/or coaches.
3. Limit warm-up pitches to five.
4. Brush the plate between innings and at any other time when needed.
5. Keep the field clear of debris, bats, loose material and spectators.
6. Keep "on deck" batter ready in designated waiting area.
7. Suspend or discontinue play when the field or weather conditions present a hazard.

Figure 11.2
Base umpire position.

Base Umpire

The base umpire renders all decisions at bases except those made by the plate umpire. In addition, the base umpire assists the plate umpire in enforcing the rules.

Position

Because of the differences in leadoff and base stealing rules between slow- and fast-pitch softball, the positions of base umpires vary somewhat. Details of these differences can be found in official umpiring manuals. Proper position of the base umpire changes with varying playing situations. When no one is on base, the umpire should stand 10 to 15 feet beyond the first base with the right foot beside the foul line in foul territory. If the ball is hit to the left side of the infield, the base umpire moves to fair territory 10 to 15 feet from first base and slightly outside of the first to second base path facing first base. If the batter-runner advances toward second base, the base umpire moves toward the inside of the infield and stays with the runner. Generally, if the ball goes outside the infield, the base umpire must go inside of the base path, and if the ball stays inside of the infield, the umpire stays outside of the base path. If the ball is hit to the outfield, the umpire moves to a spot about 5 feet to the infield side of the base line between first and second base.

With runners on first base, the umpire moves to a position between first and second base, outside of the base path. The base umpire needs to maintain a position that allows good perspective of both the pitcher and base runners. It is imperative that the position assumed does not obstruct the vision of an outfielder or impede the movements of an infielder. On a tag play, the umpire should be within 5 feet of the play and focus attention on the baseman, not the base.

Do you know where to stand to umpire bases when a runner is on first base? if a ground ball is hit to the left side of the infield? if the batter-runner advances toward second base?

Practice

Most organizations that sponsor or control league or tournament play provide clinics and workshops designed to develop and improve umpiring. The Amateur Softball Association and the National Association for Girls' and Women's Sports promote clinics, provide detailed information about umpiring, and offer programs for official ratings. Attending these events and assisting in less competitive games are excellent ways to improve ability in umpiring.

Signals

Most single decisions are indicated with both a visual and verbal signal.

UMPIRE SIGNALS

Situation	Verbal Signal	Visual Signal
Begin or resume play	Play ball	Motion to pitcher.
Strike	Strike	Raise right hand upward.
Ball	Ball	No arm signal.
Give count	Call balls first	None.
Foul balls	Foul ball	Extend arm horizontally away from diamond.
Fair ball	None	Extend arm in a pumping motion toward the diamond.
Out	None	Raise right arm and hand over right shoulder with fingers closed.
Safe	None	Extend both arms diagonally in front of body with palms facing the ground.
Suspension of play	Time	Extend both arms above his head.
Delayed dead ball	None	Extend left arm horizontally.
Trapped ball	None	Same as safe.
Ground rule double	None	Extend right hand above head with two fingers extended.
Home run	None	Extend right hand with closed fingers above head and circle arm in clockwise direction.

Can you demonstrate the umpire's visual signals for the following situations: foul ball, safe, trapped ball, home run?

Scorekeeping

The scorekeeper should have a thorough knowledge of the rules and techniques of the games, ability to make decisions, and attend to details.

The duties of the scorekeeper are to keep all records of each game as outlined in the official rules. It is the scorer's responsibility to officially determine playing

Figure 11.3
Scorekeeper.

errors, base hits, runs batted in, pitching credit for winning or losing, stolen bases, passed balls and wild pitches. The scorer shall not make decisions that conflict with official playing rules or with the umpire's decisions.

Scoresheet

The scoresheet must be completed so that it is possible to reconstruct the official action of the game from which a box score and summary of the game can be prepared. There are many ways to record official action in a game. Some scorekeepers construct their own systems. Any system may be used providing game action is accurately recorded and can be retrieved by other readers.

Each player's name and the position or positions played shall be listed in the order in which he/she batted or would have batted. In fast pitch the DH is optional, but if one is to be used, it must be made known prior to the start of the game and listed on the score sheet in the regular batting order. Ten names will be listed, with the tenth name being the player playing defense only. The same is true for the EH in slow pitch; however, all players will bat but the eleventh player will not play on defense.

Box Score

The box score should include each player's name and position and order of batting. The following information shall be recorded for each play: batting and fielding records including times at bat, runs, base hits, putouts, assists, entry and errors.

Figure 11.4
Scoresheet.

Summary

The summary of the game shall list the following information:

1. The score by innings and the final score.
2. The runs-batted-in and by whom hit.
3. Two-base hits and by whom hit.
4. Three-base hits and by whom hit.
5. Home runs and by whom hit.
6. Sacrifice flies and by whom hit.
7. Double plays and players participating in them.
8. Triple plays and players participating in them.
9. Number of bases on balls given by each pitcher.
10. Number of batters struck out by each pitcher.
11. Number of hits and runs allowed by each pitcher.
12. The name of the winning pitcher.
13. The name of the losing pitcher.
14. The time of the game.
15. The names of the umpires and scorers.
16. (FP ONLY) Stolen bases and by whom.
17. (FP ONLY) Sacrifice bunts.

First Inning

Smith was walked (BB). Jones hit a grounder to the third baseman (5) who threw out Smith at second base on a double play (4) who tossed out Jones at first base (3). (Join Smith's and Jones' boxes with a line ⊢————⊣.) Smith ① Jones ② were out. (Outs are marked by number with a circle.) Beck singled to right field (1 β). Grub hit a home run (H β) over the center field fence (note line indicating area). Two runs were batted in by third baseman number 6, which is marked by (6). Heity hit a fly ball to center field 8̂ for the third out ③. Two runs, 2 hits. 2/2.

Second Inning

Borg doubles (2 β) to left field. Grace singles (1 β) to right field, batting in Borg who had stolen third base (SB). Run batted in for Grace (3). Dotty struck out for the first out (K) ①. Near was safe at first base on an error by the first baseman who dropped the throw from the third baseman (AF, E3D). Grace advanced to second base on a fielder's choice (FC). Marion sacrificed Grace to third base (Sa¢). Smith grounded to the shortstop who threw Grace out at home plate ②. Smith was safe at first base on a (FC). Jones fouled out ③ to the first baseman (f3). One run, two hits. 1/2.

Third Inning

Beck singles to left field (1$\cancel{B}$). Grub tripled to right field (3$\cancel{B}$) scoring Beck. Run batted in for Grub (6). Grub scored on a wild pitch (WP). Heity popped out to the third baseman $\widehat{5}$ for the first out ①. Borg was hit by a pitched ball ($\cancel{H}$P). Grace hit a grounder to the second baseman who throws out Borg at second base ②, 4–6, on a throw to the shortstop who throws out Borg at first base to complete a double play ③, 6–3. Two runs, two hits. 2/2.

References

National Association for Girls' and Women's Sport. *Softball Guide,* Washington, D.C.: American Alliance for Health, Physical Education and Recreation (published biannually).

Rittler, Kathy. *Official's Manual: Softball.* West Point, New York: Leisure Press, 1982.

Softball Rules Guide. Oklahoma City, Oklahoma: Amateur Softball Association (published yearly).

Umpire Rules and Case Book. Oklahoma City, Oklahoma: Amateur Softball Association (published yearly).

Questions and Answers

Multiple Choice

1. What is the major difference between fast-pitch softball and slow-pitch softball?
   a. none
   b. more offensive plan in fast pitch
   c. more offensive play in slow pitch
   d. more offensive play in fast pitch (Ch. 1)
2. How old is the game of softball?
   a. over 100 years
   b. more than 75 but less than 100
   c. more than 50 but less than 75
   d. more than 25 but less than 50 (Ch. 1)
3. Where is the best position for the second baseman to stand when no one is on the base?
   a. on second base
   b. between first and second bases, slightly closer to second base
   c. between first and second bases, slightly closer to first base
   d. between first and second bases, halfway between first and second base (Ch. 7)
4. Who is responsible for catching a fly ball falling between the infielders and outfielders?
   a. outfielders   c. whoever calls for it
   b. infielders   d. the fastest runners (Ch. 7)
5. There are less than two outs with runners on first and second base. The batter hits a fly ball to the infield. What is the decision concerning the batter?
   a. becomes a base runner   c. automatically takes first base
   b. called out   d. continues to bat (Ch. 9)
6. Where does the short fielder position himself/herself in slow-pitch softball?
   a. in the infield near second base
   b. between the left and center fielder
   c. between the right and center fielder
   d. in the infield between the shortstop and second base
   e. where the team prefers or situation warrants (Ch. 6)
7. Who backs up the catcher when there is a play at home plate?
   a. third baseman   c. first baseman
   b. pitcher   d. second baseman (Ch. 6)
8. Who should back up the first baseman when a ground ball is hit to the second baseman with no base runners on base?
   a. pitcher   c. right fielder
   b. second baseman   d. catcher (Ch. 7)

9. When playing fast pitch, where must the pitcher's feet be placed prior to pitching?
   a. anywhere on the ground
   b. both feet on the plate
   c. one foot in front of the plate and one behind
   d. both on the ground but one on the plate   (Ch. 6)
10. What position should the infield be playing when there is a runner on third base with less than two outs?
   a. back position   c. close position
   b. halfway position   d. bunt position   (Ch. 7)
11. When may both fast- and slow-pitch base runners advance to the next base but with liability to be put out?
   a. after a fly ball is caught   c. after ball leaves the pitcher's
   b. after a base on balls   hand
                                   d. anytime   (Ch. 9)
12. Who must wear batting helmets?
   a. all adult fast-pitch and Junior Olympic fast- and slow-pitch offensive players
   b. all players in both fast- and slow-pitch softball
   c. only fast-pitch players
   d. no one, since it is optional   (Ch. 2)
13. In fast pitch, where should the third baseman stand when a bunt is expected?
   a. on base path from second base
   b. halfway from third base to home plate
   c. one third in from base to home plate
   d. more than halfway from third base to home plate   (Ch. 7)
14. What regulations distinguish slow-pitch from fast-pitch softball?
   a. moderate speed and at least a 6-foot arch
   b. no difference
   c. no deception
   d. at least a 6-inch arch.   (Ch. 6)
15. What position should the infield be playing when there is a runner on first base and less than two outs?
   a. back position   c. close in position
   b. halfway position   d. bunt position   (Ch. 7)
16. Where should a right-handed player attempt to contact the ball to place hit to right field?
   a. opposite the body   c. behind the body
   b. in front of the body   d. doesn't matter   (Ch. 4)
17. Which procedure should be followed to pitch an upshoot or rise in fast-pitch play?
   a. snap wrist right   c. snap wrist down
   b. snap wrist left   d. snap wrist upward   (Ch. 6)
18. What name was given to softball when it was first developed?
   a. Kittenball   d. Bat ball
   b. One old cat   e. Slow pitch   (Ch. 3)
   c. Rounders
19. Where is the Softball Hall of Fame located?
   a. Peoria, Illinois   b. Oklahoma City, Oklahoma
   c. Boston, Massachusetts   d. Orange, California   (Ch. 3)

20. In slow-pitch play, the batter bunts on a 1–1 count the ball in fair territory. What is the umpire's decision?

  a. batter is out   c. a strike is called

  b. foul ball   d. a ball is called   (Ch. 9)

21. In fast-pitch play, the base runner leaves the base before the non-pivot foot crosses the front edge of the pitcher's plate. What is the umpire's decision?

  a. legal, base runner is safe

  b. illegal, base runner is out

  c. illegal, ball is called on the batter

  d. depends on what the batter does to the pitch   (Ch. 9)

22. A batted ball bounces in the infield and then rolls outside the base line. What is the decision of the umpire?

  a. strike   b. out   c. fair ball   d. foul ball   (Ch. 9)

23. What is the minimum number of innings to be completed for an official game?

  a. seven   c. four

  b. six   d. five   (Ch. 9)

24. The batter has one strike and two balls when he/she tips the next pitch, which is caught by the catcher. What is the decision of the umpire?

  a. strike   b. out   c. fair ball   d. foul ball   (Ch. 9)

25. The catcher drops the ball on the third strike. Bases are full and there is one out. What is the umpire's decision?

  a. strike   b. out   c. foul ball   d. ball   (Ch. 9)

26. What is the umpire's signal for suspending play?

  a. extend both arms above the head

  b. raise right hand upward

  c. extend both arms diagonally in front of body

  d. extend arm in a pumping motion   (Ch. 11)

27. What action should a right-handed batter take to place hit the ball to left field?

  a. contact ball opposite body and follow through naturally

  b. contact the ball a little past the center of body and follow through toward right field

  c. contact the ball anywhere over the plate and swing fast with a full follow-through

  d. contact the ball in front of the body, "break" wrists sharply to cause a forceful follow-through   (Ch. 4)

28. Where is the strike zone for fast-pitch softball?

  a. between the shoulders and ankles and over the plate

  b. no higher than the neck and no lower than the knees and over the plate

  c. between armpits and knees over the plate

  d. between armpits and the knees   (Ch. 1)

29. What should a fielder do to avoid running into a fence when catching a fly ball near it?

  a. reach for fence with non-glove hand

  b. reach for fence with glove hand

  c. look back for the fence while moving back

  d. concentrate only on catching the ball   (Ch. 5)

30. How many bases may a base runner advance on an overthrow over the third baseman's head into fair territory?

  a. one   b. two   c. as many as possible   d. none of these   (Ch. 4)

31. What action should be taken to correct a tendency to strike out by missing the ball?
    a. shorten grip and watch the ball closely
    b. shorten grip and adjust stride
    c. lengthen grip and swing faster
    d. lengthen grip and adjust stride   (Ch. 4)
32. Which fast-pitch delivery makes a complete circle for the windup?
    a. straight pitch   b. slingshot   c. windmill   d. rocker   (Ch. 5)
33. Where do the coaches stand to help the offense?
    a. anywhere in foul territory   b. they must sit on the bench
    c. by the manager   d. on the sidelines by first and
                                              third base   (Ch. 10)
34. What is the correct movement for a right-handed person in executing an overhand throw?
    a. stand with left shoulder toward person to whom the ball is going and step ahead on the left foot
    b. stand with the left shoulder toward the person to whom the ball is to be thrown and step ahead on the right foot
    c. stand facing the person to whom the ball is to be thrown and step ahead on the left foot
    d. stand any way that is comfortable and step ahead on either foot   (Ch. 5)
35. Where should the hands usually be placed on the bat?
    a. both hands close together at the end of the bat
    b. hands separated about 2 inches apart, but near the end of the bat
    c. hands separated, about 3 inches from end of the bat
    d. hands close together about 2 or 3 inches from the end of the bat   (Ch. 4)
36. Which is the correct method to use in fielding ground balls?
    a. wait for the ball to roll to you
    b. run forward to meet the ball and try to field it on the first bounce
    c. run forward to meet the ball, but wait until the ball has slowed down to assist in stopping it
    d. creep up on the ball slowly.   (Ch. 5)
37. How should a fielder catch a fly ball that is going over his/her head?
    a. run backwards and keep eye on the ball
    b. wait until the ball has landed and then run to pick it up
    c. let the player behind you catch it
    d. turn around and run toward the direction the ball is headed, keep eye on the ball   (Ch. 5)
38. How should the batting order be selected?
    a. let the team decide
    b. according to the positions played on the team
    c. according to the batting skill of the batters
    d. pitcher, catcher, then the weakest hitters next   (Ch.7)
39. What is the term used for a weak fly that lands safely?
    a. Bobbie   c. Texas Leaguer
    b. Chopper   d. Frozen Rope   (Ch. 3)
40. Which grip on the bat will provide the most power?
    a. long   c. choke
    b. medium   d. depends on the batter (Ch. 4)

41. What action listed below will help to correct hitting only ground balls?
    a. swing up on the ball   b. swing down on the ball
    c. swing level at the ball   d. swing harder at the ball (Ch. 4)

42. How should the batter adjust his/her position when the ball leaves the pitcher's hand?
    a. relax   c. shift weight to rear foot
    b. hold position   d. shift weight to forward foot
                                           (Ch. 4)

43. When playing fast-pitch softball, which type of pitch is easiest to bunt? (Right-handed batter)
    a. high outside   d. low inside
    b. low outside   e. high inside   (Ch. 4)
    c. in the middle

44. What is the correct method to round a base?
    a. swing wide before reaching the base and touch any part of the bag
    b. run straight to the base, touch the inside corner and pivot body around
    c. curve out a bit several feet from the base and touch the inside corner
    d. get there any way possible   (Ch. 4)

45. Which slide provides the smallest tag area?
    a. straight-in   c. hook
    b. bent-leg   d. headfirst   (Ch. 4)

46. Which slide is best to avoid being tagged?
    a. straight-in   b. bent-leg   c. hook   d. any of the above   (Ch. 4)

47. What position should your hands be in to field or catch a ball below your waist?
    a. thumbs together   c. left hand only, palm up
    b. little fingers together   d. hand with glove on it, facing
                                     upward   (Ch. 5)

48. What is the correct position for fielding a ground ball? (Right-handed player)
    a. brace feet apart with left foot ahead, bend knees and hips
    b. bend only from the waist
    c. brace feet apart with right foot ahead, bend knees and hips
    d. bend from knees and hips only   (Ch. 5)

49. What is the best body position for a tag play?
    a. straddle the bag, place gloved hand in front of base
    b. stay to one side of base and tag runner
    c. brace feet apart behind the base and reach for the runner
    d. block the base with the left foot and tag the runner   (Ch. 5)

50. What is the advantage of a sidearm throw?
    a. the throw can be done faster
    b. more accurate for a short distance
    c. speed and power are best
    d. throw can be delivered sooner   (Ch. 5)

TRUE OR FALSE

51. Softball playing field dimensions for pitching, infield and outfield size vary depending upon the type, level and gender of play. (Ch. 1)
52. Legal bats can be made of plastic. (Ch. 2)
53. Pitchers have priority over all fly balls that travel across several positions in the infield. (Ch. 7)
54. The first option of the defensive players involved in a rundown play is to outrun and tag out the base runner. (Ch. 6)
55. In 16-inch slow-pitch play the pitcher may attempt to pick off a base runner who is leading off. (Ch. 9)
56. A passed ball is a pitched ball that the batter does not attempt to swing at. (Ch. 3)
57. Managers are in charge of the team. (Ch. 8)
58. A foul ball and a foul tip are the same thing. (Ch. 3)
59. It is legal for the pitcher to start to pitch and then stop. (Ch. 3)
60. Game play is the major goal of softball practice. (Ch. 8)
61. If the pitcher hits the batter with a pitched ball, the batter is allowed to go to first base. (Fast-pitch play) (Ch. 9)
62. The only time a base runner must be tagged out is when he/she is forced to run. (Ch. 9)
63. If a base runner is hit with a batted ball, he/she is out immediately. (Ch. 9)
64. Base runners may run outside the base path to avoid being tagged. (Ch. 10)
65. Designated hitters (DH) are permitted only in slow-pitch play. (Ch. 4)
66. Short fielder play in the infield or outfield. (Ch. 6)
67. All official softballs are 12 inches in circumference. (Ch. 2)
68. There are special playing rules for co-ed softball. (Ch. 9)
69. The ASA is the official rule-setting agency. (Ch. 9)
70. An "extra hitter" is eligible in fast pitch. (Ch. 4)
71. An outfielder should throw toward an infielder for a possible cutoff when a batter gets a hit with runners on base. (Ch. 5)
72. Imagining a perfect swing or throw is a helpful psychological technique to improve performance. (Ch. 10)
73. Stealing a base is permitted in all types of softball play. (Ch. 4)
74. You should never change your mind while in the act of sliding. (Ch. 7)
75. When no one is on base, the catcher should back up the first baseman on throws to third base. (Ch. 7)
76. Slow-pitch pitchers try to deceive batters by varying the height of the arc and hitting the corners of the plate. (Ch. 6)
77. Catchers should always hold their mitt as a target in the middle of the plate. (Ch. 6)
78. "Giving" with the catch will prevent the ball from bouncing out of the glove or hands. (Ch. 5)
79. The palm of the hand should be on the ball for proper direction of the ball for a good throw. (Ch. 4)
80. When catching a ball thrown to a base with an advancing runner, catching position should be delayed to the last second. (Ch. 5)

Completion

81. What techniques can help a player to concentrate? (Ch. 10)
82. What is the term applied to the catcher and pitcher? (Ch. 3)
83. What is the name of the organization that promotes softball in the United States? (Ch. 2)
84. What is the offensive play called when the base runner tries to advance at the same time the batter tries to hit the ball? (Ch. 4)
85. What two types of bunts are executed to achieve a base hit? (Ch. 4)
86. What is the term applied to a play that is interrupted or intercepted enroute to the intended receiver? (Ch. 5)
87. Who covers home plate on a wild pitch with a runner on third base? (Ch. 5)
88. What should fielders do to shield their eyes from the sun if they have no sunglasses? (Ch. 5)
89. What kind of a hit will a level swing produce? (Ch. 3)
90. What action must be applied to the swing to deaden the ball for bunting? (Ch. 4)
91. List three factors that would determine whether you should steal a base while playing fast-pitch softball. (Ch. 4)
92. What are the two main purposes of executing a cutoff throw? (Ch. 6)
93. List three kinds of pitches. (Ch. 6)
94. Where should the outfielders play when a powerful right-handed batter is batting? (Ch. 7)
95. What is the difference between a safety and a suicide squeeze? (Ch. 7)
96. What is the term applied to gaining two outs on one batted ball? (Ch. 3)
97. What is the major purpose of a slide? (Ch. 4)
98. What conditions influence rule variations for softball play? (Ch. 11)
99. What is the visual signal that an umpire gives to indicate a "ball?" (Ch. 11)
100. What is the name of the tenth player in fast-pitch softball who does not play defensively? (Ch. 1)

Question Answer Key

Multiple Choice

1. c	6. e	11. a	16. c
2. a	7. b	12. a	17. d
3. c	8. d	13. d	18. a
4. a	9. d	14. a	19. b
5. b	10. c	15. b	20. a

21. b	26. a	31. a	36. b
22. d	27. d	32. c	37. d
23. d	28. c	33. d	38. c
24. a	29. a	34. a	39. c
25. b	30. c	35. d	40. a

41. c	46. c
42. c	47. b
43. b	48. a
44. c	49. a
45. d	50. c

True or False

51. T	57. T	63. T	69. T	75. T
52. T	58. F	64. F	70. F	76. T
53. F	59. F	65. F	71. T	77. F
54. T	60. F	66. T	72. T	78. T
55. T	61. T	67. F	73. F	79. F
56. F	62. F	68. T	74. T	80. T

Completion

81. self-talk and imagery
82. battery
83. ASA
84. hit-and-run
85. drag and push
86. cutoff
87. pitcher
88. use glove
89. line drive
90. give
91. speed, no. of outs, kind of batter, ability of defense, score
92. to stop the runner from advancing and to throw out a base runner
93. curve, drop, fast, rise, knuckleball, change-up
94. back to left
95. The third baseman can return to third base on a safety squeeze but must continue to run to home plate on a suicide squeeze.
96. double play
97. avoid tag
98. age, gender and type of play
99. none
100. designated hitter

Index

Altered bat, 16
Amateur Softball Association (ASA), 2, 7, 8,
  10, 14–16, 107, 113, 120
American Alliance for Health, Physical
  Education, Recreation, and Dance,
  11
American Physical Education Association, 14
Angle bunting, 27
Anquillare, John, 15
ASA. *See* Amateur Softball Association
  (ASA)
Assist, 16
Away, 16

Backing, 69
Backing patterns, 96–97
Back position, 94
Backstop, 16
Back-up, 16, 80, 86, 97
Bag, 16
Baker, John "Cannonball," 15
Balk, 16
Balls, 8
Balls and Strikes, 120
Base on balls, 16
Basepath, 16
Baserunning, 32–40, 91–92
Baserunning regulations, 111–12
Bases, 10
Bases full, 16
Bases loaded, 16
Base umpire, 126
Bats, 7
Bat swinging, 23–25
Batter, 2, 3
Batter's box, 16
Battery, 16
Batting, 21–32, 89–90
Batting order, 16, 90
Batting regulations, 111
Batting tee, 31
Bean ball, 16
Beat out, 16
Blocked ball, 16
Blooper, 16

Bobble, 16
Box, 16
Box score, 17, 128–29
Bunt, 17
Bunting, 26–29, 90
Bunt play position, 94

Castle, Tom, 15
Catch, 17
Catcher, 72–77
Catcher's box, 17
Center fielder, 84
Chambers, Jim, 15
Change of pace, 17
Change-of-pace pitch, 67
Chicago Farragut Boat Club, 13
Choke, 21–22
Chopper, 17
Chucker, 17
Circuit clout, 17
Class organization, 104
Clean the bases, 17
Cleanup, 17
Close position, 94
Coaching, 92
  duties, 104–5
  teaching, and managing, 101–6
Co-ed play, 4, 113
Competitive play, 119–20
Conditioning, 102, 118–19
Conduct, of game, 104, 115
Count, 17
Covering, 69, 76, 95–97
Covering the base, 49, 76, 80
Crane, Ben, 15
Crowd the plate, 17
Cummings, Bill, 15
Curtis, Jerry, 15
Curveball, 67
Cut, 17
Cutoff, 17, 77, 81, 98
Cutoff throws, 57–58, 70
Cycle, 17

Dead ball, 17
Defensive patterns, 93–98
Defensive position play, 63–88
Defensive positions, 2–3
Defensive skills, 41–60
Defensive stations, 3
Deliveries, 64–66
DeLuca, Frank, 15
Designated hitter, 2, 17
Diamond, 3, 17
Dobson, Margaret, 15
Doubleday, Abner, 13
Double play, 17
Down, 17
Drag bunting, 28
Drop, 67

Earned run, 17
Earned run record, 71
Elliott, Sam, 15
Equipment, 4
    selection and care, 7–10
Error, 17
Evaluation, 32, 51, 60, 71, 82
Extra-base hit, 17
Extra hitter, 17

Fair ball, 17
Fake bunting, 29
Fan, 17
Fast-pitch pitching, 63–69
Fast-pitch softball, 2–3, 9, 14
Fielder's choice, 17
Fielding, 41–48, 75–77, 93–95
Fielding record, 82, 88
First baseman, 77
Fischer, Leo H., 13
Fleece balls, 8
Fly balls, 17, 43–45, 87
Foot in bucket, 18
Footwork, mimetic, 81
Force out, 10
Foul ball, 18
Foul lines, 2
Foul tip, 18
Four bagger, 18
Free trip, 18
Full count, 18
Fungo, 18

Game
    playing the, 110
    and rules, 107–13
    sample, 114
Gears, Harold, 15
Gerber, Warren, 15

Gloves, 8
Grand slam, 18
Grayson, Betty, 15
Grip, 21, 53, 68
Groove, 18
Ground balls, 45–47, 76
Grounders, 2, 3, 18

Hakanson, Walter A., 13
Halfway position, 94
Hall of Fame. *See* National Softball
        Hall of Fame
Hancock, George W., 1, 13
Helmets, 4, 8
Hi Ho Brakettes, 14
Hit, 18
Hit-and-run, 22, 25
Hit away, 18
Hit batsman, 18
Hitters, 90
Hit the dirt, 18
Holding runners, 86
Hole, 18
Home plate, 10
Hopkins, Ida, 15
Hot corner, 18
Hunter, John, 15

Illegally batted ball, 18
Illegally caught ball, 18
Imagery, 119
Infield, 2, 18
Infielders, 77–83
Infield fly rule, 18
Infielding, problems and corrections, 81
Innings, 18
Instruction, 103
Intercollegiate associations, 10
Interference, 18
International Joint Rule Committee on
        Softball, 107
ISC. *See* International Softball Congress, 11,
        16, 120

Johnson, Hugh, 15
Joyce, Joan, 15
Junior Olympic, 4
Justice, Charles, 15

Kampschmidt, Bernie, 15
Keystone sack, 18
Kirkendall, Dizzy, 15
Korgan, Nina, 15

Language, of softball, 13–20
Law, Marjorie, 15
Laws, unwritten, 114–15

142   *Index*

Lay one down, 18
Leading off, 92
Lead off, 18, 36–38
Leadoff, 18
Left fielder, 84
Linde, Al, 15
Line drive, 18
Lopiano, Donna, 15
Lore, of softball, 13–20

Managing, teaching, and coaching, 101–6
Masks, 4, 9–10, 14, 18
May, Gloria, 15
Miller, Clarence, 15
Mimetic footwork, 81
Mimetic pitching, 70
Mitts, 8

NAGWS. *See* National Association for Girls
	and Women's Sports (NAGWS)
National Association for Girls and Women's
	Sports (NAGWS), 11, 113
National Association for Intercollegiate
	Sports, 107
National Association for Sport and Physical
	Education, 11
National Collegiate Athletics
	Association, 107
National Federation of High School
	Activities Association, 12
National Recreation Association, 14
National Softball Hall of Fame, 11, 15
Nutritional conditioning, 119

Obstruction, 19
Offensive patterns, 89–93
Offensive skills, 21–40
Official rules, 113–14
Officiating, 113
Olympics, 10
One Old Cat, 13
Organization, 120
Out, 19
Outfield, 2, 19
Outfielder evaluation form, 83
Outfielders, 83–88
Outside pitch, 19
Overhand snap, 55
Overhand throw, 54
Overrun, 19
Overthrow, 19

Pan American Games, 10
Pass, 19
Passed balls, 19
Patterns of play, 89–99
Pauley, M. J., 13

Pepper, 32
Peralta, Amy, 15
Pete's Hideaway Whips, 14
Physical conditioning, 118
Picking off, 77
Pickoff, 19
Pinch hitter, 19
Pinch runner, 19
Pitcher, 2, 3, 63–72
Pitcher's plate, 10
Pitches, types of, 67–68
Pitching
	fast-pitch, 63–66
	grips, 68
	mimetic, 70
	problems and corrections, 71
	rules, 64, 110
	slow-pitch, 64
Pitching regulations, 64
Pitchout, 19
Pivot and throw, 82
Pivotfoot, 19
Place-hitting, 24–25
Planning, 101
Plate umpires, 124–25
Play
	competitive, 117–20
	patterns of, 89–100
Players, and substitutes, 110
Playing, the game, 117–20
Playing field, 107–9
Pop flies, 76
Pop-ups, 19
Porter, Don, 10
Position play, defensive, 63–88
Pregame warmup, 102
Preplan, 57
Preseason conditioning, 102
Priority plays, 98
Protectors, 4, 9–10
Protest, 19
Psychological conditioning, 119
Pulled-in position, 93–94
Pull hitter, 19
Push bunting, 28
Putout, 19

Ramage, Jim, 15
Ramsey, Lorene, 15
Rating chart, 83
RBI, 19
References, 5, 12, 20, 40, 61, 88, 99, 105,
	116, 121, 131
Reinhardt, Myron, 15
Relay man, 19

Index   143

Rich, Kay, 15
Right fielder, 85
Rise, 67
Rober, Lewis, 13
Ropp, Don, 15
Rounders, 13
Rules
    of game, 107–14
    official, 113–14
    and pitching, 64
Run batted in, 19

Sacrifice bunt, 19
Sacrifice fly, 19
Sacrificing, 26–29
Safety, 29, 50, 58, 70, 87, 105
Sample game, 114
Scorekeeping, 114, 127
Scoresheet, 128
Scratch hit, 19
Sears, Ruth, 15
Second baseman, 79
Self-evaluation, 117
Self talk, 119
Shin guards, 4
Shoes, 10
Shoestring catch, 19
Short fielder, 85
Shortstop, 79
Sidearm throw, 56
Signals, 74
    umpire, 127
Sims, Alberta, 15
Sioux City Penn Corporation, 14
Sixteen-inch slow pitch, 113
Skills
    defensive, 41–62
    offensive, 21–40
Sliding, 34–36
Slingshot, 64–67
Slow pitch, sixteen-inch, 113
Slow-pitch pitching, 69
Slow-pitch softball, 2, 4, 9, 14
Softball
    game today, 10–12
    history, 1–2
    language and lore, 13–16
Softball Hall of Fame. *See* National Softball
    Hall of Fame
Softball Insight, 120
South Florida Club, 14
Southpaw, 19
Spooks, 14
Spring, John, 15
Squeeze, 19
Squeeze bunt, 19

Stance, 22–23, 41–42, 73
Starpath-Kink's Glass, 14
State High School Associations, 120
Stealing, 19, 38–39
Steele's Silver Bullets, 14
Stephenson, Ray, 15
Sterkel, Harvey, 15
Straight away, 19
Straight pitch, 65–67
Strategy
    and baserunning, 37
    team, 94
Stuff, 19
Substitutes, 92
Swing, 23–26

Tag, 19
Tag play, 49–50
Target, 74–75
Teaching, coaching, and managing, 101–6
Team organization, 104
Team selection, 102–3
Team strategy, 94
Texas leaguer, 19
Third baseman, 80
Three bagger, 20
Throat protector, 4
Throwing, 53–58, 75–76, 86
Thrown balls, 47–48
Tickey, Bertha, 15
Town Ball, 13
Trap, 20
Trapping the runner, 81
Triple play, 20
Two bagger, 20

Umpire signals, 127
Umpiring, 123–31
    pregame duties, 124
    signals, 127
Underhand pitch, 56
Underhand toss, 56
Uniforms, 4
United States Slow-Pitch Softball Association
    (USSPSA), 10
Unwritten laws, and rules, 114–15
Upshoot pitch, 67
USSPSA. *See* United States Slow-Pitch
    Softball Association (USSPSA)

Wadlow, Marie, 15
Wait out, 20
Walk, 20
Warmup, 104
Warm-up bats, 118
Watson, Paul "Windmill," 15

Weighted balls, 118
Weighted bats, 118
West, Bill, 15
Wild pitch, 20
Windmill, 64–65, 67
Win-loss record, 71
Women's Professional League, 14
Wrigley, P. K., 121
Wrist snap bats, 119